NEW ORLEANS
Proud to Call It Home

INTRODUCTION BY
Pete Fountain

ART DIRECTION BY
Bob Kimball

SPONSORED BY
Young Leadership Council

TOWERY PUBLISHING
a division of Baretz Publishing, LLC

New Orleans
Proud to Call It Home

Contents

URBAN
TAPESTRY
SERIES
TOWERY
PUBLISHING

A DIVISION
OF BARETZ
PUBLISHING, LLC

By Pete Fountain

You'll never hear laughter as genuine or as rich as in
New Orleans.

That's part of what makes New Orleans the special place that it is.
The people have a wonderful sense of humor, and because of it, you
just fall in love with the spirit of the place right away. Life is different here—it's better somehow—and the laughter of the people lets
you know that. They're saying that they're proud of New Orleans—
its heritage and its lifestyle.

And, sometimes, they're saying that they know how to cope with bad
things as well. The weather, for instance, is something you need to be
able to laugh at. Most of the year it's fine, but you come down here in
July or August and it's just murder. People come here from places like
Vegas, where they know from the thermometer that it's really hot, and
they get off the plane and just die. Our humidity hits them, and no
matter how hot it is back home, they just can't believe it. But we put
up with it, and after a while, even the visitors get to where they pay
no attention to it. They, like the rest of us, laugh at it.

For me, New Orleans is all about the people who live here. It's not
like other places, where everybody keeps their distance. The people
here really want to get to know you. If you get in some trouble, or
have a hard time, they really want to help you. They have a warmth
about them that you just don't find in too many other places. Most
of them truly love their city, and whether you ask them or not, they
want to tell you what makes it so special.

What I want to do—using my life's love of music as an example—
is to tell you just what it is that I think makes New Orleans such
a terrific place. I want to tell you why it is that I've spent my life
here—playing my clarinet, getting to know lots and lots of people,
and doing a whole lot of laughing in the process. ▶

It's well known that New Orleans people have a way of enjoying life. A lot. We make an art form out of living, and we're not afraid to share our art form with anyone. The result is that it's like New Year's Eve every night down in the French Quarter, with people celebrating the art of being alive, and celebrating their love of the city and its culture.

For me, the celebration began when I was just a little kid. This was during the Great Depression, when there wasn't much else to do but hang out in the neighborhood with your pals and, if you were lucky enough to have a couple of nickels, go to the movies and see an all-day series of matinees and serials and cartoons.

As I got a little older, and was in school, I started going to the movies at night with my friends. I remember that when I'd walk down to the movie house—the Arcade Theater—I would pass a kind of indoor-outdoor club where you could stand outside and hear the big bands playing New Orleans music. It was in the air, literally.

So as I grew, I came home later and later, and before I knew it, I was leaving the movies about 10 o'clock, but I wouldn't get home until about 1 or 2 in the morning. I had been sitting outside these dance halls—one in particular was the Top Hat Dance Club—so that I could hear the headliners, who naturally played the late gig on the bill.

What I was hearing was jazz. New Orleans jazz, pure and simple. Some of it was big-band jazz. Most of it, though, was pure New Orleans jazz played by the classic six- or seven-piece New Orleans band: three melody instruments (usually trumpet, clarinet, and trombone) and three or four rhythm instruments (drums, bass, guitar or banjo, and piano).

At this particular time I heard Louis Prima playing at one place, and his brother Leon Prima playing at another. Then there was Sharkey Bonano, a trumpet player who had a really good little band. As a matter of fact, I played with his band later on. ▶

Well, I was hooked. I had started playing the clarinet when I was nine, right before World War II. Five years later, when I was only 14, I started playing professionally. There I was, a teenager, and I was hanging around the clubs in the early 1940s and listening to all the music that was going on around New Orleans at the time. It was my passion and my education all at once.

Well, OK, it didn't really happen all at once. Things just seem that way in hindsight. There was, of course, the war going on at the time, and work wasn't that steady for musicians. I used to hang out at a place on Broad Street called Peterson's Music Store, about a block and a half from where I lived. Whenever the professionals would come to town to play a gig, they'd all come by Peterson's. When he knew they were coming, Mr. Peterson would make me run home and get my clarinet, and then he'd make me play for the professionals. And that's how I really built up my chops. Playing for the "real" musicians built me up to where I could play really well.

Mr. Peterson had a little jazz band himself—the Broad Street Social and Pleasure Club, he called it—and I played in that. We'd do little parades. New Orleans is known for its parades; you give somebody a flag and a drum, and you've got a parade. When the guys in the band needed some money, they'd stop by my house and pick me up and we'd do a parade around the neighborhood. We'd get a beer barrel, a couple of drums, and a flag, and we'd start a parade—playing New Orleans jazz and making a little money in the process.

My mother wasn't too crazy about that because I was supposed to be doing my lessons, my schoolwork. But this is how I really got my education. I never did get into studying classical clarinet music, although I do love it. But I had a high school teacher who realized I was going to play New Orleans music no matter what, so he encouraged me in that direction. It was a great act on his part, because it gave me the boost I needed to go straight from Mr. Peterson's little band, and the parades, right to the "Conservatory of Bourbon Street" when I was about 14. ▶

And that's where I really did my formal training as a jazz musician.
So there I was, playing jazz music on Bourbon Street when I was in
high school. I was out late almost every night doing that—making
$120 a week, too, which was pretty good money for a kid to be
bringing home back then. But even though it was hard for me to
make it to class, this one teacher who had encouraged me to pursue
my dream and go play this New Orleans music probably realized
that it was in my blood and nobody was going to take it out of me.
It wasn't all kindness on his part, I'm sure. He was a gorilla of a man,
and maybe he just didn't want anybody sleeping in his class. Whatever
the reason, it was a blessing to have such encouragement and
support at that age and at that stage of my career.

During that part of my life, a whole world opened up to me—
personally, culturally, and spiritually. And the world that opened
was New Orleans music. I had been playing it for four or five
years, and I had been listening on the way home from the movies.
But until I started playing with the real jazz players down on Bourbon
Street, where it all began, I wasn't really a part of it.

All that changed in a hurry, though. I've already mentioned how the
spirit of the people of New Orleans is reflected in their laughter—
in their sense of humor and their goodwill. But if the spirit of the
people and the city is really reflected in anything, it's got to be in the
music. The music reflects the whole way of life here, because this
is where so much American music was born. Jazz led into the blues,
which led into rock and roll, and they all shared the stage with gospel
and sacred music. And it all started right here—coming from New
Orleans and helping to make the city what it is.

You can see this, and hear this, in all the old jazz players from a
hundred years ago—Jelly Roll Morton and Sidney Bechet and, of
course, the greatest, Louis Armstrong. And you can still hear it in the
young musicians, guys like Harry Connick Jr. Or in the whole Marsalis
family—Ellis, the father, who's a terrific pianist and teacher; Branford,
who plays sax; and Wynton, who plays trumpet and is the artistic

director of Jazz at Lincoln Center in New York. The whole family
plays and they're all terrific. Sometimes I've thought that it just
doesn't seem fair to have that much talent in one family.

But that's New Orleans in a nutshell, because they're all wonderful
people as well. It's just a really special place, and the music both
reflects the special qualities and is formed by the special qualities,
so that you get everything all rolled up together.

And so I consider myself to be lucky to have been a part of this, and
to have been able to have my career unfold right here in New Orleans.
The only time I had to be away from New Orleans for an extended
period was when I went on the road for two years with Lawrence
Welk, back in the 1950s. That's what made me a national personal-
ity—it's when people across the country first heard me play the
clarinet. But it damn near killed me because he wouldn't let anybody
drink. It was a tough two years for a guy who had cut his chops on
Bourbon Street, I guarantee.

Still, I don't want to sound like I'm not grateful for the opportunity
that came from the national exposure, because it really gave me a
national podium for promoting New Orleans music to the world.
And, after a couple of years, it gave me a chance to come back to
New Orleans and open my own club down in the French Quarter.
First it was at 800 Bourbon Street, and then I moved up to 231
Bourbon Street. Now, for the past 25 years, I've been in the Hilton.

The French Quarter is really a magic place. Jackson Square could be
in the middle of a French town somewhere—you'd never know the
difference. The French Quarter is the spiritual heart of the city, where
the rhythm of New Orleans originates. The buildings, some of which
date back to the 1700s, are enchanted and enchanting. It's a magical
place, like a living museum where the spirits of the past come alive. It
does get pretty rowdy down there at night—and during Mardi Gras,
forget about it—and some folks might be put off by that. But if that
lifestyle isn't for you, there are lots of daytime charms: shops and

restaurants, carriage rides and streetcars, and café au lait and those wonderful beignets at the Café du Monde. This is where you can get a historical tour of old New Orleans without having to do a whole lot of walking.

You can also get great meals at some of the best restaurants in the world. No list is ever going to be comprehensive or complete, but just a few of their names ought to make your mouth water: Brennan's, Arnaud's, the Acme Oyster House, Dominique's, Galatoire's, K-Paul's, and Pere Antoine's. And that's just the French Quarter we're talking about. Throughout New Orleans—from the Commander's Palace in the Garden District to Bozo's in Metairie to Prejean's up in Lafayette— you've got some of the best chefs and the best restaurants in the world.

You put it all together—the people, the music, the atmosphere, the food, the love of life—and living in New Orleans is like being in another country. It's like going to France (or, in places, Spain or Portugal or Greece), but still being able to understand the people. Well, maybe that's going too far. There are plenty of visitors who would argue that you can't understand a word of what people down here say. The Cajun-inflected, Deep South accent comes off the tongue a little thick—sounding a bit like a Brooklyn accent— but when you start to listen, you realize it's like nothing else in the country. Still, you can understand us if you try.

Music, food, heritage, love of life, a special outlook on the world— sure, other cities have some of these elements. I don't want it to sound like New Orleans has a monopoly on them. But the difference is that we really do have them all here. And when you have them all in one place, it makes the city really something. It makes the music come alive. It makes the people's laughter joyous and genuine. And it makes New Orleans the best city in the world. ●

I T HAD TO BE THEM: TERM LIMITS restrict Mayor Marc H. Morial (LEFT) to eight years at the city's helm, but during his tenure, the popular New Orleans leader cleaned up police corruption and set his sights on revitalizing his hometown. His Rebuild New Orleans Now! capital program has shoveled millions of dollars into refurbishing the cityscape, from recreational facilities to roads. For Harry F. Connick (OPPOSITE), who has served as the city's district attorney since 1973, primary areas for study and action include an increasing emphasis on providing assistance to victims of crimes.

FOR PEOPLE THE WORLD OVER, the very name "New Orleans" suggests a place rife with mystery and a unique melding of cultures. Catching and holding the glow of the sun, the city's Central Business District—CBD—rises toward the sky in proud acknowledgment of its reputation. The CBD contains the majority of the city's high-rises, including One Shell Plaza (ABOVE, IN CENTER), the tallest office building in Louisiana.

AT JACKSON SQUARE, IN THE heart of the French Quarter, St. Louis Cathedral captures the souls of aspiring artists while tending to those of its parishioners. New Orleanians have held religious services on the site since 1727, and the current structure—completed in 1794—is the official seat of the Archdiocese of New Orleans.

S OME GENTLEMEN PREFER blondes; others aspire to emulate them. Bedecked and bedazzling, the Big Easy is home to retail giants and funky shops whose wares draw a bead on patrons' various and sundry needs.

NEW ORLEANS

FOUNDED IN 1718 AND NAMED for a French regent, New Orleans feels its historical French connection deeply. Joan of Arc's crucial contribution to freeing France from British rule in 1429 is immortalized by the equestrian *Maid of Orléans* (OPPOSITE), perpetually victorious in the French Quarter. Street performers, too, shine as living illustrations of how Joan of Arc captivates the city's collective imagination (LEFT).

NEW ORLEANS

IN A CITY KNOWN FOR ITS ROUND-the-clock hubbub, one sure source of repose is New Orleans' statuary. The bronze figures frozen in time at Woldenberg Riverfront Park (OPPO-SITE) enjoy an eternal view of the Mississippi River. At Lee Circle—the crossroads of the Central Business and Warehouse Arts districts—K&B Plaza (PAGES 30 AND 31) showcases an impressive corporate collection of contemporary sculpture by such greats as Henry Moore, Louise Bourgeois, Isamu Noguchi, Elizabeth Frank, and Barbara Hepworth.

NEW ORLEANS

INDING ALONG THE BANKS OF the Mississippi River between New Orleans and Baton Rouge, the River Road is dotted with historically and architecturally lavish plantations. At Nottoway Plantation, the Great White Ballroom (LEFT) is just one of more than 60 rooms in the mansion, which was one of the first to feature the innovation of indoor plumbing. San Francisco Plantation (OPPOSITE TOP), completed in 1856, melds Old Louisiana Colonial style with vibrant colors that catch visitors' eyes—much like the quarter-mile lane of namesake trees at the 1839 Oak Alley Plantation (OPPOSITE BOTTOM).

Peaceful and inviting Longue Vue House and Gardens, just minutes north of downtown, was originally the home of philanthropists Edgar Bloom Stern—a cotton broker—and his wife, Edith, an heiress to the Sears Roebuck fortune. The Classical Revival mansion's 45 rooms retain their original antique furnishings and modern art collection, and eight acres of constantly blooming gardens offer plenty of nooks for quiet interludes.

Monteleone

AT A HOST OF ORNATE INNS throughout the city, visitors to New Orleans can steep themselves in eras past. Statues representing peace and prosperity flank the entrance to Le Pavillon Hotel (LEFT), completed in 1907 and listed on the National Register of Historic Places. Located in the Vieux Carré, or Old Square—better known outside the city as the French Quarter—the Hotel Monteleone (OPPOSITE) has welcomed guests since 1886.

NEW ORLEANS' ARCHITECTURAL and cultural evolution is reflected in and by its buildings, from sleek glass structures to neat row houses standing in the shadows of formal stone behemoths.

AMERICAN DOMINATION
1803–1861
1865 TO DATE

THE CONFEDERATE STATES OF AMERICA · 22 FEBRUARY 1862

DEO VINDICE

CONFEDERATE DOMINATION
1861–1865

No matter who holds the reins of power, New Orleans has always been pointedly its own. Memorials around the city serve as poignant reminders of those who fought for their country's freedom.

IN MEMORY OF THE
AMERICAN AND ALLIED
ARMED FORCES
WHO BRAVELY FOUGHT
AND SACRIFICED
DURING THE VIETNAM WAR

NEW ORLEANS

On June 6, 2000—the 56th anniversary of D-Day—The National D-Day Museum first opened its doors to the public and celebrated the culmination of a dream for many, including Donald T. "Boysie" Bollinger, chairman of the museum's board (OPPOSITE BOTTOM). The facility's New Orleans location was selected as a tribute to Andrew Higgins, a New Orleanian who designed the Landing Craft Vehicle Personnel that allowed Allied forces to land on an open beach. Comprising two buildings—a renovated warehouse and the Louisiana Memorial Pavilion (OPPOSITE TOP)—the museum's theater and exhibit spaces salute different aspects of this pivotal moment in world history.

GREATER NEW ORLEANS IS PA-trolled and protected to the fullest extent of the law by the New Orleans Police Department (ABOVE) and the Jefferson Parish Sheriff's Of-fice, under the command of Sheriff Harry Lee (OPPOSITE). A colorful local figure and the state's first Chinese-American sheriff, Lee has been in office since 1980.

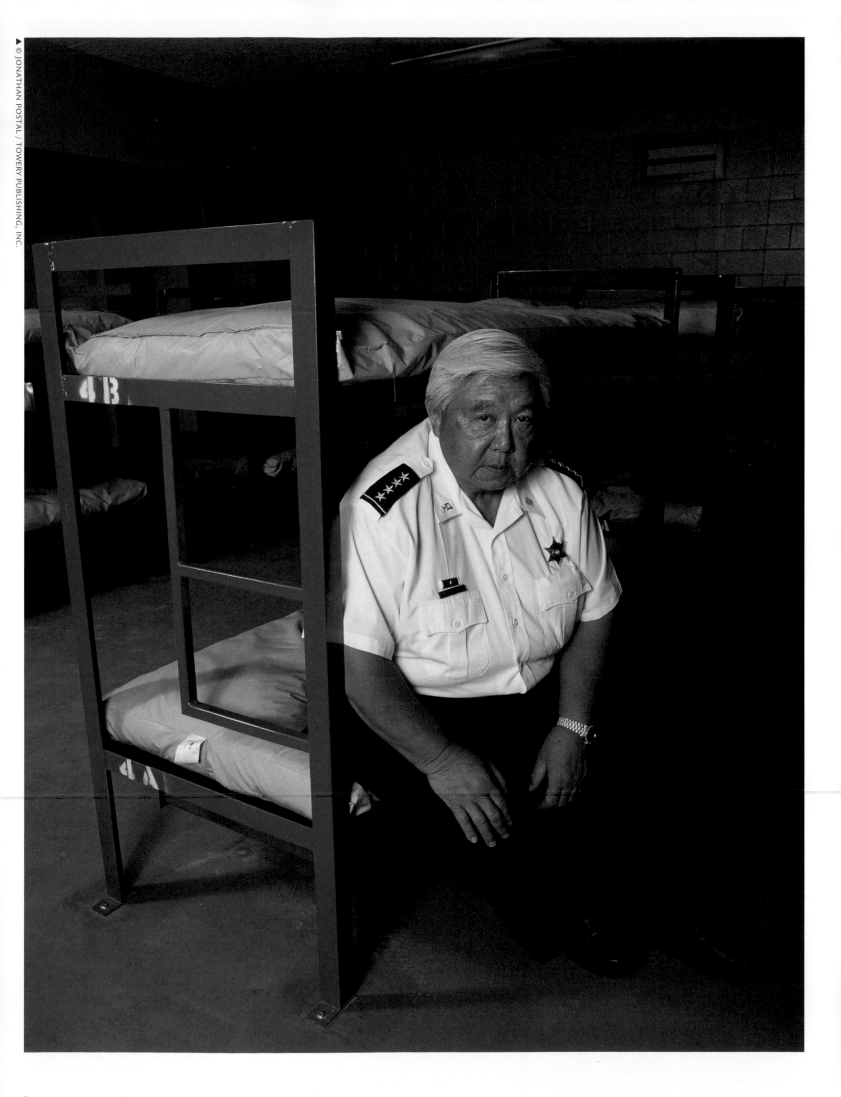

NEW ORLEANS

I N THE HEAT OF THE MOMENT, members of the New Orleans Fire Department can be found in the thick of things, battling flames, smoke, and fumes to save lives and property. Established in 1829 as the Firemen's Charitable Association, the group be-came a paid department in 1891.

I T'S EASY TO BECOME IMMERSED in New Orleans, where rushing fountains like the one dominating Spanish Plaza (OPPOSITE) soothe the senses and cool the sweat of the brow.

Mysterious and compelling, cities of the dead—New Orleans' above-ground cemeteries—are far more than the sum of their parts. Fulfilling the needs of the living as well as those of the departed, St. Roch Cemetery's chapel (ABOVE) houses a niche lined with gifts of thanks left by those who have been healed of various afflictions.

NEW ORLEANS

EXPRESSIONS OF HOPE AND thanks are evident on a grand scale in New Orleans. The 14 decorated columns of the Robert and Annette Bloch Cancer Survivors' Plaza (OPPOSITE), ensconced in the Central Business District, stand as an enduring testament to people winning fights against the disease.

Funeral processions jazz up the streets when those involved in the Crescent City's music scene have sounded their final notes. Featuring somber processions to gravesides and joyous recessionals from them, jazz funerals have been held for luminaries such as (FROM OPPOSITE LEFT) Charlie Bering, who owned the legendary Lu and Charlie's jazz club and served as the New Orleans Jazz and Heritage Festival's contemporary jazz coordinator; Louisa "Blue Lu" Barker, whose singing-songwriting career spanned nearly three-quarters of a century; and world-renowned jazz clarinetist and saxophonist Albert "Pud" Brown.

NEW ORLEANS

Fʀᴏᴍ ʜᴇᴀᴠᴇɴ ᴏʀ ꜰʀᴏᴍ Eᴀʀᴛʜ, proof of New Orleanians' respect for their ancestors is visible at a number of the city's more than 40 cemeteries. Offerings of food and flowers left at loved ones' final resting places stand as tributes to the departed.

BLARNEY STONE
RECOVERED AND RESTORED
TO ITS RIGHTFUL LOCATION
1 OCTOBER 1994

THE ABILITY TO SPEAK FLUENT blarney is a rare gift, but those who have it are likely to turn others green with envy—the perfect color for the enormous annual St. Patrick's Day parade in New Orleans' Irish Channel neighborhood. At Tulane University, processions of students regularly touch the school's miniature Blarney Stone (OPPOSITE) for a little Irish luck before exams. The stone, which disappeared from the uptown campus for several months in 1994, now graces Tulane's Engineering Square.

NEW ORLEANS

© JONATHAN POSTAL

© JEFF STROUT / STROUT PHOTOGRAPHY

RESIDENTS OF NEW ORLEANS turn out en masse at Christmas-time, when everything from bon-fires and garlands of lights to stars like native son John Goodman (LEFT) combine to illuminate the season.

BUILDING DREAMS: VISITORS to Blaine Kern's Mardi Gras World can view—and have their picture taken in front of—some of the most famous carnival props ever made. In 1947, Blaine Kern Sr. (OPPOSITE) produced a single float for a lone Mardi Gras parade, thus hand-carving the foundation for Kern Studios. Now employing some 100 people, his company produces more carnival floats than any other establishment in the world, and also populates theme parks and other venues with its trademark colorful figures.

During Mardi Gras, dragons and other fanciful creatures take over the roads. The 140-foot Leviathan float (ABOVE) is one of the centerpieces of the star-studded Krewe of Orpheus, cofounded by entertainer Harry Connick Jr. (OPPO-SITE TOP) in the 1990s and named for the storied musician of Greek myth. The less-well-known faces that make up the Society of St. Ann (PAGES 66 AND 67) are an otherworldly but familiar part of an unofficial Mardi Gras parade in the French Quarter.

New Orleans

PROUD TO CALL IT HOME

PROCESSION OF PLUMES: The crowds that make up annual Mardi Gras celebrations include the various peaceful tribes of the Mardi Gras Indians. African-Americans dressed in painstakingly theatrical garb, members of these groups honor the Native Americans who took in escaped slaves.

NEW ORLEANS

EADS UP: HUNDREDS OF EYES peer at and beckon to window-shoppers in the Big Easy. Though some of these visages may seem familiar, their main political agenda is to persuade passersby to become potential purchasers.

NEW ORLEANS

THERE ARE ARTISTS WHO FIND that the sidewalks provide the broadest audiences for their work. On any given day, in any corner of the city, pedestrians may be serenaded or otherwise drawn into the constant work in progress that is New Orleans.

WHETHER GRAVE OR EXUBER-
ant, shaped by bone or carved
from stone, denizens of New
Orleans go blue in the face casting
their expressive light over the city.

HE WITCHING HOUR IS ALWAYS close at hand in New Orleans, which may help explain the preoccupations of best-selling novelist Anne Rice (BOTTOM). Many of the Crescent City native's books are set in her hometown, touring local landmarks around which characters appear and fade away in accordance with the author's almost supernatural will.

CURSES FOILED AGAIN: VOODOO priestess Ava Kay Jones—who also holds a degree in law—has been called upon to perform numberless ceremonies since 1989, when she became a full-time priestess. In 2000, for her most well-publicized assignment to date, Jones was hired by officials of the New Orleans Saints to attempt to lift a curse affecting the football team at its home stadium, the Superdome.

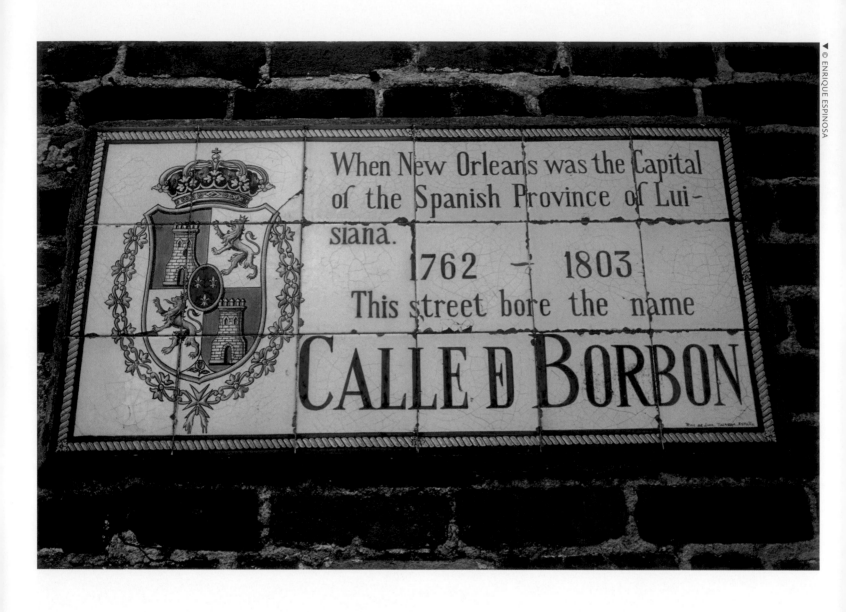

When New Orleans was the Capital of the Spanish Province of Luisiana. 1762 — 1803 This street bore the name

CALLE D BORBON

For legions of visitors to New Orleans, the French Quarter's Bourbon Street is regarded as the edgy center of the city's reputation for excitement. Although many of the shops now lining the road are of the traditional tourist variety, signs of history are still intact, quenching the thirst of those cruising the thoroughfare.

IN ADDITION TO BETTER-KNOWN types of dogs, New Orleans is home to its own special mutation: the highly sought-after purple pooch. During Mardi Gras, some humans show their good breeding by dyeing their dogs in royal hues and donning complementary coiffures.

THE STREETCAR NAMED DESIRE makes an annual five-day stop in the Big Easy, when the Tennessee Williams/New Orleans Literary Festival assumes center stage. The celebration of the arts takes place in the French Quarter—near residences once occupied by Williams—and the event's performances, literary tours, and competitions include the Stanley and Stella Shouting Contest (OPPOSITE), won in 2001 by Guy Schaafs (ABOVE).

SINCE 1911, THE NEOCLASSICAL structure that houses the New Orleans Museum of Art—NOMA—has been recognized as a work of art in its own right. The facility, located in the middle of lushly treed City Park, safeguards nearly 40,000 items in its permanent collections. NOMA's holdings range from an extensive photography collection and a history of Louisianan art to a gallery featuring silver and glass.

FILLED WITH BUILDINGS THAT have been transformed into apartments and art galleries, the city's burgeoning Warehouse Arts District paints a broad swath across the canvas of New Orleans. Creative folk having brushes with fame include musician and artist Tony Green (OPPOSITE, TOP LEFT), whose murals grace walls around town even as notes from his gypsy jazz guitar fill the air. The iconographic oil paintings of Dimitri Fouquet (OPPOSITE, TOP RIGHT) perpetuate an aura of mystery, and native son Terrance Osborne (OPPOSITE BOTTOM) has had some of his acrylics featured on MTV's *Real World 9*, set in New Orleans.

NEW ORLEANS

HISTORY IS IN THE MAKING AND eccentricity is in the eye of the beholder for people as far-flung as Jae Weise of the downtown vintage shop Retroactive (OPPOSITE) and John Preble of the UCM—Unusual Collections & Minitown—Museum in Abita Springs. A short drive north of New Orleans, the UCM is literally a world of its own, cobbled together from bizarre combinations of found objects, old buildings, and animated exhibits.

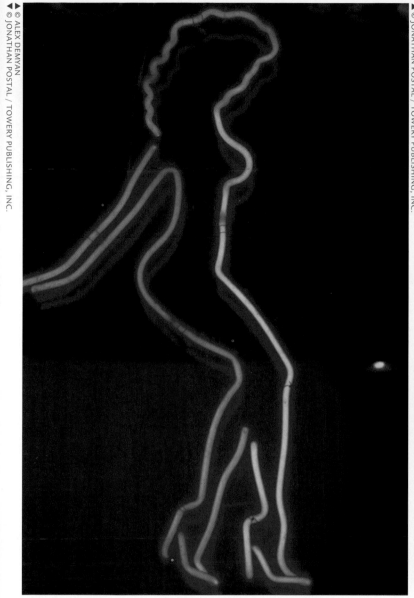

SHOWGIRLS ARE ALIVE AND WELL in the French Quarter, thanks in large part to the legendary Chris Owens, owner and star of the Chris Owens Club (OPPOSITE). Owens has been dancing, singing, and otherwise lighting up her audiences' nights for decades. Making the most of a good thing, the 20-woman Shim Shamettes strut their stuff at the Shim Sham Club during shows celebrating burlesque's heyday. The group includes (ABOVE, FROM LEFT) Lily Valley; assistant director and choreographer Nina "Boom Boom" Boomavitch; and Lorelei Lane, choreographer, director, and producer.

NEW ORLEANS

Sᴘɪɴɴɪɴɢ ᴛʜᴇ ʀᴇᴄᴏʀᴅs, ᴡᴇᴀᴠ-ing the music: On Tuesday nights, Lewis White (ᴏᴘᴘᴏsɪᴛᴇ) lets his passion for music play itself out over the airwaves as he hosts WWOZ 90.7-FM's *Jazz from the Park*. For professor and New Orleans-style jazz clarinetist Dr. Michael G. White (ʟᴇꜰᴛ), the music he hears is as important as the music he makes. His 2000 album, *A Song for George Lewis*, pays homage to the musician whose musical inflections inspired White's own style.

AGE HAS NOTHING TO DO WITH getting into the swing of things in New Orleans. Bringing the audience to its feet has been a longtime goal for Johnny Angel (OPPOSITE, IN CENTER) and his band, the Swingin' Demons. A regular attraction at venues around town, the group has donated its time and talents to a ballroom's worth of fund-raisers.

PROUD TO CALL IT HOME

Bowling isn't everyone's bag, but Mid City Lanes Rock 'N' Bowl, owned by John Blancher (ABOVE), is in a league of its own. The 18-lane bowling alley frames its easygoing atmosphere with live zydeco, blues, swing, or other music nearly every night, and performers such as Geno Delafose and his band French Rockin Boogie (OPPOSITE, TOP RIGHT) and drummer Leo Thomas (OPPOSITE, BOTTOM RIGHT) score strike after strike with the venue's patrons.

O NCE A LINK BETWEEN LAKE
Pontchartrain and the Mississippi
River, Bayou St. John fronts
the residential Faubourg St. John—
New Orleans' oldest neighborhood—
near City Park. With several homes
dating from the early 19th century,
the area houses layers of memories.

NEW ORLEANS RESERVES A SPE-
cial font of affection for its children, whether they're dressed for
special occasions or for a hard day's
play in one of the city's many parks.

THE STRUCTURES THAT HOUSE New Orleans' centers for higher learning are nearly as impressive as the schools themselves. Tulane University (RIGHT) traces its roots back to 1834, when it was founded as the Medical College of Louisiana. Since then, Tulane has expanded its curriculum and enrollment, and is now attended by a total of nearly 12,000 undergraduate and graduate students each year. Just a few minutes from the French Quarter, Loyola University New Orleans (OPPOSITE) counts residents of every state in the country—and nearly 50 other nations—among its students. Consistently ranked as one of the top schools in the region, Loyola offers a liberal-arts education set within a Jesuit framework.

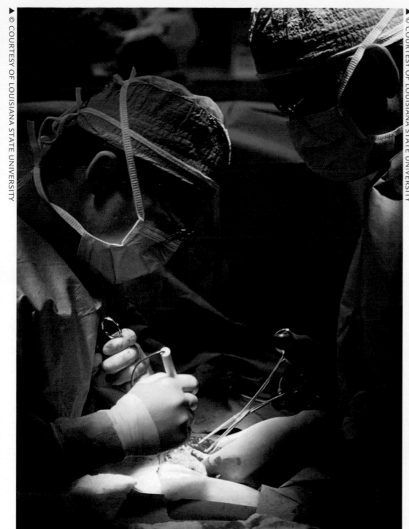

Since it was established in 1931, the Louisiana State University Health Sciences Center has operated as an institution offering rigorous training. The New Orleans facility's offerings include schools of dentistry, medicine, and nursing; in addition, the school stresses the importance of patient care and community outreach as part of the education process, and maintains a number of clinics in the city.

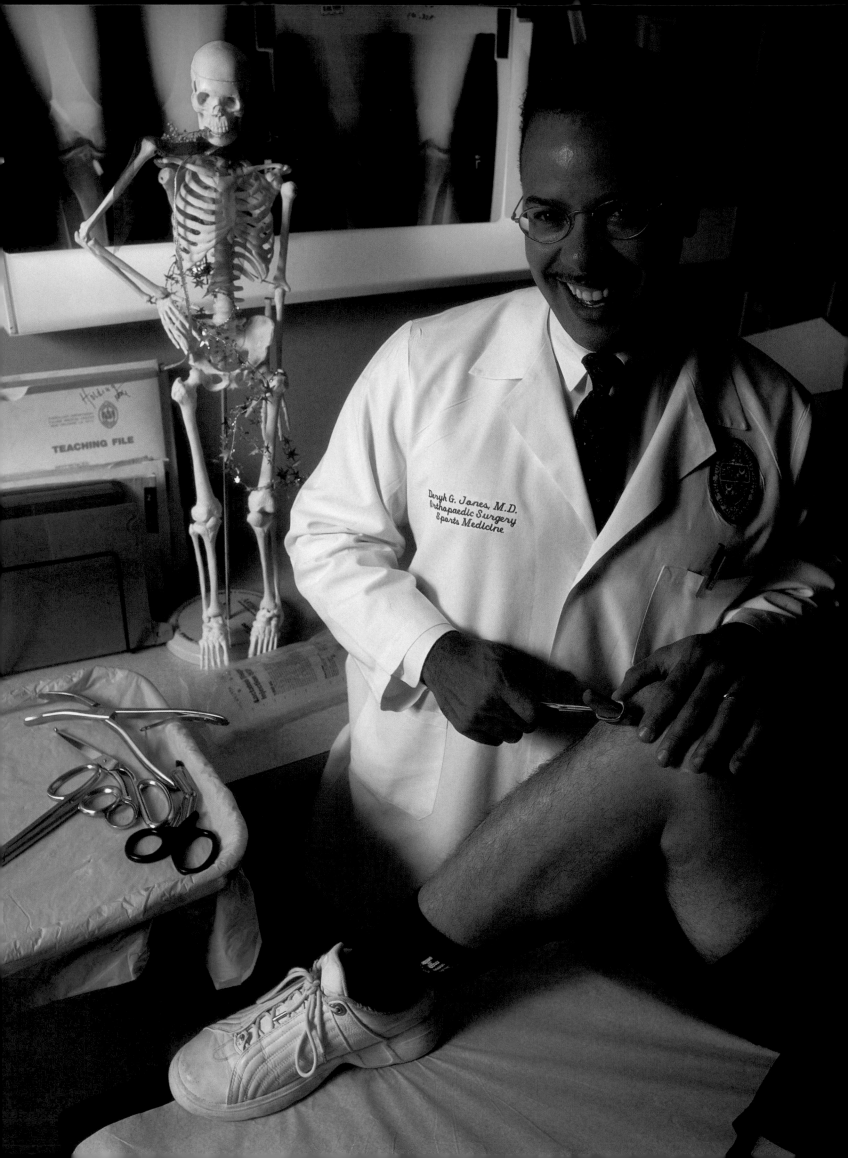

NO PAIN, NO GAIN: SPORTS aren't just fun and games for athletes and the doctors who tend to their various injuries. Steve Cheredaryk of New Orleans Brass Hockey (ABOVE) may play defense, but he's on the offensive when sticking it to the competition. Repairing damaged bodies is reflexive for Deryk G. Jones, M.D. (OPPOSITE), an assistant professor of orthopedic surgery at the Tulane Institute of Sports Medicine—the official health care provider for the Brass.

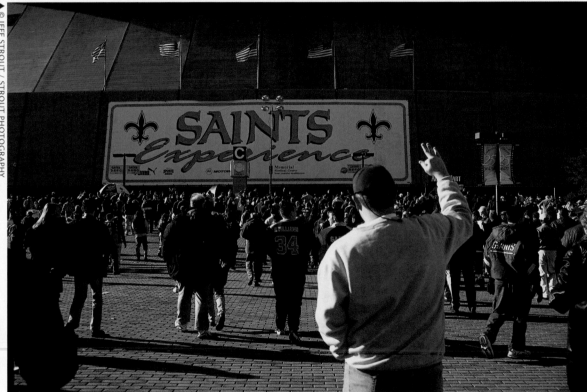

EXCITEMENT REIGNS SUPREME AT the Superdome, whether it's the New Orleans Saints or the Tulane University Green Wave who go marching in. Dominating 52 acres of the Central Business District's turf, the multipurpose arena is on the ball when it comes to hosting football and basketball games, concerts, annual shows, and other events.

EVERY SPRING, THE NEW Orleans Zephyrs blow back into town like a breath of fresh air. The Triple-A affiliate of the Houston Astros, the Zephyrs—including pitcher Travis Driskill and mascot Boudreaux—regularly draw in excess of 400,000 fans per season to Zephyr Stadium.

NEW ORLEANS

SNAKES ALIVE: HOP ON A STREET-car or board a boat to Audubon Zoological Garden. The zoo, located in Audubon Park at a bend in the Mississippi River, is just a short, scenic distance from both the French Quarter and the Central Business Dis-trict. Residents of the zoo include sea lions, elephants—and some reasonable facsimiles thereof—and other tradi-tional animals, as well as rare white alligators that keep an eye on visitors checking out the Louisiana Swamp Exhibit.

ITH ITS BAYOUS, LAKES, and proximity to the Gulf of Mexico, the New Orleans area is a natural when it comes to providing spots for fishing, whether for compliments or for supper. With hundreds of thousands of Louisianians holding recreational fishing licenses—and other species catching their own share of finned food—rods, reels, and fishing boats play a central part in the region's economy.

PROUD TO CALL IT HOME

STORMY WEATHER: NEW ORleans' natural beauty transcends calm water and clear days. Even ominous waterspouts and flashes of lightning can strike a chord in the hearts of viewers, although watching wild weather from anyplace outdoors may indicate clouded judgment.

I T TAKES A SHARP EYE TO KEEP a lookout for friends and foes alike. From dorsals at the Audubon Aquarium of the Americas (TOP) to sailboats bobbing on Lake Pont- chartrain (OPPOSITE), New Orleans offers nautical angles for man and man's best friend.

NEW ORLEANS

Proud to Call It Home

THE SHIPPING NEWS: BETWEEN its location at the mouth of the Mississippi River and its position as an inland waterway link to the American Midwest, clear economic skies are assured for the Port of New Orleans (OPPOSITE). The port is one of the busiest in the country, with more than 22 million square feet leading the way in imported coffee, steel, and natural rubber; exports range from oil and petrochemicals to rice and corn.

When the feet grow weary and driving becomes tiresome, a short local cruise can be a lifesaver. The paddle wheeler *Creole Queen* offers daily jaunts around the harbor, as well as more lengthy dinner jazz cruises. Making several round-trip runs every day between Audubon Zoo and the Audubon Aquarium of the Americas, the riverboat *John James Audubon* also provides hands-on educational exhibits.

NEW ORLEANS

THERE'S SOMETHING FOR EVERY-one to sink their teeth into at the Audubon Aquarium of the Americas, which rises at the riverfront edge of the French Quarter. Housing more than 10,000 water-loving crea-tures, the aquarium's exhibits also include a miniature replica of an Amazon rain forest.

WHEN THE FESTIVAL OF FINS first swam into New Orleans in 2000, the gaudily painted fiberglass objects peppering streets and businesses may have looked fishy to some residents. Each piece was decorated by a different local artist, and when the fish were auctioned off, a school of local charities hooked more than half a million dollars.

New Orleans

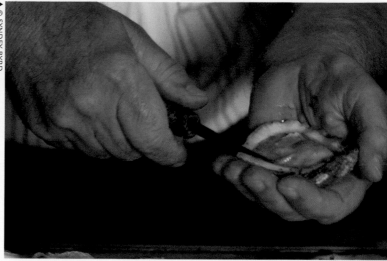

WHEN THE DESIRE FOR PURE New Orleans cuisine—whether oysters or gumbo—makes itself known, stores and restaurants, including those in the French Market, are happy to satisfy that hunger. Stretched along the riverfront in the French Quarter, the market's shops include the world-famous Café du Monde, serving its trademark beignets and chicory-laced coffee around the clock.

FROM FIELD TO TABLE, NEW Orleans presents a cornucopia of fresh food and places to enjoy it. All the ingredients for a stomach-stretching meal—and a centerpiece for the table—are available at the Crescent City Farmers Market, a not-for-profit project of the ECOnomics Institute at Loyola University. Those putting in their time at the market include (OPPOSITE, FROM LEFT) Richard McCarthy, the ECOnomics Institute's executive director, and market President Sharon Litwin, who also sows and reaps the benefits of local talent as executive director of the Louisiana Philharmonic Orchestra. For people who prefer making reservations to preparing meals, the city offers a taste of the good life with its full menu of fine restaurants. At the Central Business District's 56 Degrees, Executive Chef Minh Bui (LEFT) presides over the creation of contemporary American cuisine with a strong Asian influence. Ella Brennan (RIGHT), co-owner of Commander's Palace in the Garden District, carries on the traditions that have made the restaurant the toast of the town—and a name known around the world—for more than a century.

CRAWFISH ARE A SPECIALTY OF the house in Louisiana, appearing as everything from appetizers to full meals and jewelry. The spiny lobster's popularity prompts hundreds of the annual crawfish festivals that are staples of the region.

Bam! The colorful Chef Emeril Lagasse (opposite) opened Emeril's—the first of his three popular New Orleans restaurants—in 1990, but began achieving the lagniappe of international recognition when his earliest televised cooking show heated up network ratings in 1994. In the French Quarter, award-winning Chef Susan Spicer of Bayona (left) prepares Mediterranean-based dishes with exotic twists. And just a short drive north of the city, the Abita Brewpub (right) offers diners the chance to talk with the brewers while enjoying their meals and sampling Abita's beers and soft drinks.

PARADE REGALIA KEEPS FESTIVE New Orleans figures frozen in time. But as the city's nightlife takes wing, regulars belly up to the bar at watering holes around town to enjoy a deep swig of the Big Easy.

New Orleans

THE CITY KNOWN LOCALLY AS N'awlins speaks a rich language all its own—part French, part Spanish, with a hint of African and Caribbean thrown in for good measure. Whatever might be said about the Bayou region's dialect, the signs along the way certainly don't mince words.

THE VITALITY OF NEW ORLEANS shimmers in countless ways and places: in the city's phenomenal mixture of cultures, in its vibrant neighborhoods and mingling of modern and historic architecture, in breathtaking natural landscapes—and in the very air, which seems suffused with color. For all these reasons and hundreds more, New Orleanians are proud to call their city home.

PROFILES IN EXCELLENCE

A look at the corporations, businesses, professional groups, and community service organizations that have made this book possible. Their stories—offering an informal chronicle of the local business community—are arranged according to the date they were established in the New Orleans area.

Bally's Casino

Delgado Community College

French Market Corporation

Healthy New Orleans Partnership

John A. Alario Sr. Event Center

Jones, Walker, Waechter, Poitevent, Carrère
    & Denègre, L.L.P.

Latter & Blum Inc./Realtors

McGlinchey Stafford, PLLC

McIlhenny Company

Northrop Grumman Ship Systems'
    Avondale Operations

Ochsner Clinic Foundation

Pauli's Bicycle & Fitness Store

Proud to Call It Home/New Orleans 24/7, Inc.

Prudential Gardner, Realtors

RE/MAX New Orleans Properties

Royal Sonesta Hotel and Chateau Sonesta Hotel

Taylor Energy Company

Tenet Hospitals of New Orleans

Tulane University Health Sciences Center

University of New Orleans

Whitney National Bank

World Trade Center of New Orleans

Young Leadership Council

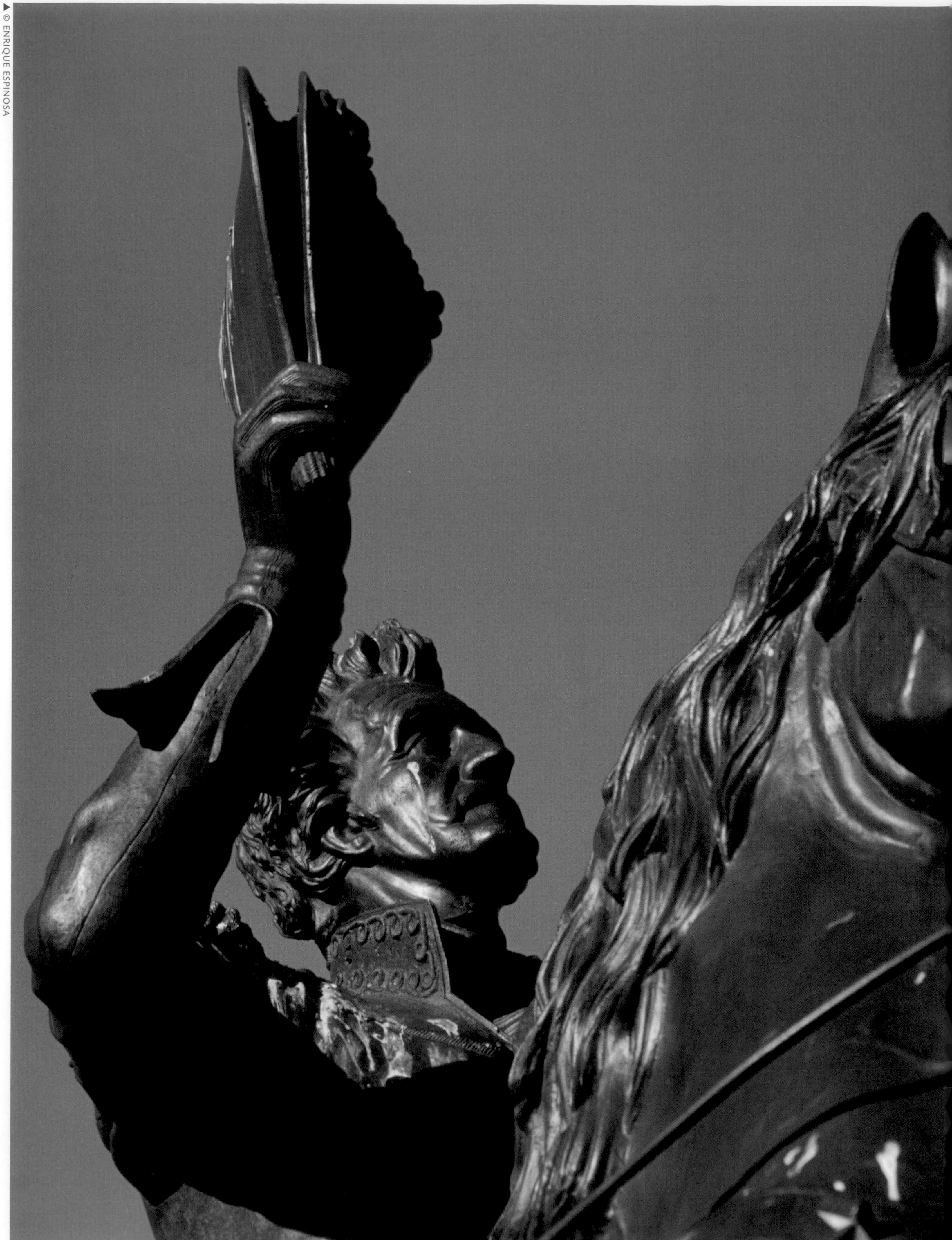

▲ © ENRIQUE ESPINOSA

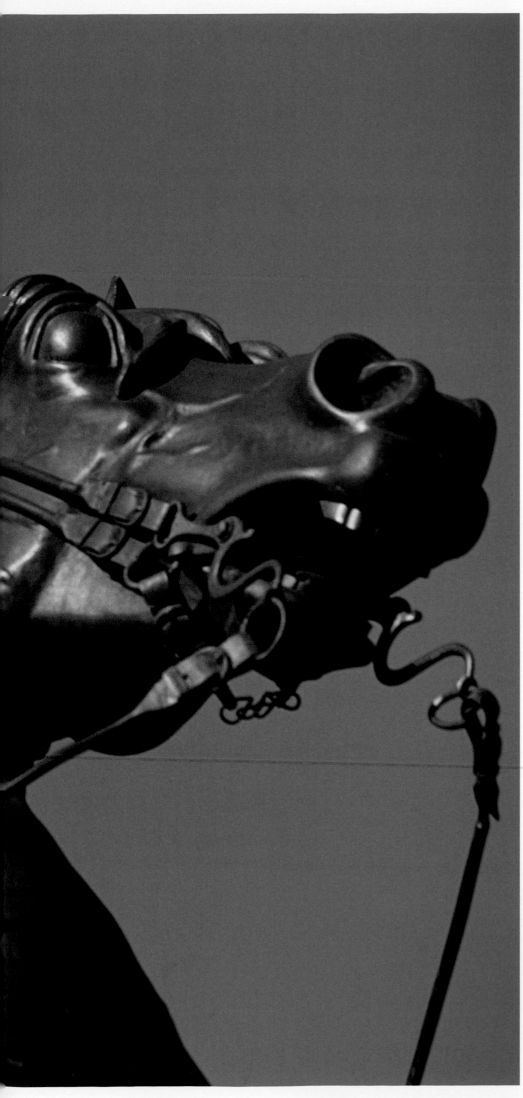

1791-1949

FOR MORE THAN 200 YEARS, THE HISTORIC FRENCH MARKET has been a symbol of pride and tradition that has captured the hearts of locals and tourists alike. Located on the banks of the Mississippi River in the French Quarter of New Orleans, the French Market originated from a Native American trading post on the site chosen for the city of New Orleans by the French in 1718.

From Café du Monde to the Farmers' Market and Community Flea Market, America's oldest continuously operated public market serves as a cultural, commercial, and entertainment hub to the Crescent City. The market continues to thrive by playing a leading role in the local economy and remaining a tradition as old as the city itself.

EARLY MARKET DAYS

Since the market's beginning in 1791, the city's best-known landmark has been a commercial and cultural melting pot, gumbo style. Despite fires, foreign wars, domestic political struggles, and numerous hurricanes, which sometimes destroyed the market's framework, the core of the market—a mecca to ships and traders—has remained a vital link to the city of New Orleans and the world.

Over the market's long history, a diverse group of frequent visitors and traders have spoken a Babel of languages. In the early days, those who frequented the "gumbo" market included Gascon butchers; Italian and Spanish fruit vendors; German vegetable vendors; Moors with their strings of beads and crosses; Chinese and Hindu; Jewish and Teuton; French and Creole Malay; Irish and English; African-Americans selling coffee, pralines, *calas,* and rice fritters; and the Choctaw Indians from north of Lake Pontchartrain, who brought varieties of herbs, spices, and crafts.

Coffee drinking played a central role in the life of the market during the 19th century. Sunday "making market" was considered a traditional family outing, and ended with a café au lait at the coffee stalls. Italians—Sicilians selling mostly fruits and vegetables—began dominating the market in the late 19th century. More than a century later, merchants and farmers of Italian heritage continue to play a leading role in the life of the market.

MITCHELL OSBORNE

TODAY'S WALKING TOUR

Today, the French Market offers upscale shopping, entertainment, and New Orleans cuisine with the atmosphere of the country's oldest continuously operated public market.

The Butchers' Market, or Halle des Boucheries, was designed in 1813 by city surveyor Jacques Tanesse to replace earlier buildings destroyed by hurricane and fire. The home of coffee stands since the 1860s, as well as the Butchers' Market, it houses the French Market's oldest tenant, Café du Monde.

In 1870, the Bazaar Market, built and designed by Joseph Abeilard, one of America's first African-American architects, had 164 stalls. However, the bazaar was destroyed by a hurricane in 1915. Rebuilt during the 1930s by the Public Works Administrations, the Bazaar Market was converted to retail shops and boutiques during the 1970s.

The Vegetable Market, or Halle des Légumes, built and designed by Joseph Pilié in 1882, contains restaurants and retail space today. The Red Stores, a row of three identical

FOR MORE THAN 200 YEARS, THE HISTORIC FRENCH MARKET HAS BEEN A SYMBOL OF PRIDE AND TRADITION THAT HAS CAPTURED THE HEARTS OF LOCALS AND TOURISTS ALIKE.

buildings built in 1833 by Manuel Simar Cucullu and Christoval G. de Armas, were partially destroyed by fire in 1840, and eventually demolished in the 1930s. The modern-day replicas were built as part of the 1970s renovation.

"It's exciting to imagine all the millions of people coming through here for 200 years," says Stephen B. Hand, executive director. "It makes you realize you're only here a short time. The market is going to continue once we're gone."

MODERN MANAGEMENT

Prior to the late 1800s, the City of New Orleans sold franchises in the market to collect rents, maintain order, and enforce sanitation. By order of Mayor Robert Maestri in 1932, the city council formed the French Market Corporation under the leadership of the French Market Business Men's Association. The corporation rehabilitated and modernized the market by rewiring antiquated electrical systems and by adding colonnades and cupolas, refrigeration, and enclosed open-air buildings.

In 1975, the French Market Corporation, under the direction of Mayor Moon Landrieu, administered a major renovation project by adding restaurants and transforming the market's open stalls into modern shops. These projects were the first step in the rebirth of the riverfront as a major attraction, since railroads and changing port technology had cut the city off from the river.

In 1978, Mayor Ernest N. "Dutch" Morial began making several dramatic physical improvements to the French Market—adding the performance tent, flood-wall gates, historic displays, and statuary. Morial also promoted commerce and entertainment in Dutch Alley. The Flea Market grew substantially by opening daily as a major shopping attraction.

Beginning in 1986, Mayor Sidney Barthelemy's leadership renovated existing French Market buildings, built a parking facility, and added more flood walls. In 1991, the market was selected to host the International Public Market Conference. In 1993, the French Market Visitor Center was built. This period also saw the birth of countless festivals, community events, and concerts held at the market.

Today, under the leadership of Mayor Marc H. Morial, the market has evolved into a financially viable organization that educates and entertains millions each year, in addition to returning considerable revenue to the city. Under Mayor Morial's supervision, the French Quarter Corporation continues to beautify and preserve the market with its French Quarter Style reform campaign.

"We're very proud that we have made the market a profitable entity," says Hand. "I don't think we need to change or grow. We need to concentrate on taking care of what's here and preserving it." ●

FROM CAFÉ DU MONDE TO THE FARMERS' MARKET AND COMMUNITY FLEA MARKET, AMERICA'S OLDEST CONTINUOUSLY OPERATED PUBLIC MARKET SERVES AS A CULTURAL, COMMERCIAL, AND ENTERTAINMENT HUB TO THE CRESCENT CITY.

IN THE EARLY 1800S, NEW ORLEANS RESIDENTS BATTLED TROPICAL diseases such as endemic malaria and annual epidemics of cholera and yellow fever. In an attempt to combat these diseases, a group of young practicing physicians founded the Medical College of Louisiana in 1834. Following the Civil War, Paul Tulane bequeathed funds to establish a new

university—Tulane University.

Today, researchers and doctors at the Tulane University Health Sciences Center (TUHSC) are becoming national leaders in education, research, and health care. The medical center provides general and specialized clinical services for the entire gulf south region, and performs groundbreaking research in such areas as HIV/AIDS, gene therapy, women's health, and environmental diseases.

A WEALTH OF INNOVATIVE PROGRAMS

TULANE UNIVERSITY HEALTH SCIENCES CENTER IS A LEADER IN HEALTH CARE, EDUCATION, AND RESEARCH.

Located in the heart of the downtown New Orleans medical district, the TUHSC campus spans 3.2 million square feet in seven high-rise buildings. The center comprises the School of Medicine, School of Public Health and Tropical Medicine, Tulane/Xavier Center for Bioenvironmental Research, Tulane Regional Primate Research Center, Tulane University Hospitals and Clinics, and the Student Health Service.

Approximately 600 students are enrolled at the School of Medicine, as well as some 600 resident physicians in more than 40 accredited training programs, 85 clinical fellows taking training following their residencies, and approximately

80 research fellows. In the School of Public Health and Tropical Medicine, some 1,400 students from more than 50 countries are pursuing graduate degrees at the master's and doctoral levels.

Tulane's School of Medicine is the 15th-oldest medical school in the country and the first established west of the Allegheny Mountains. The School of Public Health and Tropical Medicine is the oldest in the country and is home to the only department of tropical medicine in the nation. Tulane is also the only university in the South that is both ranked as a Carnegie I research university and ranked in the top quartile of research universities by the Association of American Universities. And TUHSC has the only federally designated women's health center in the South.

The School of Medicine currently has 550 faculty members and more than 1,000 physicians serving as volunteer faculty. The School of Public Health has 370 faculty members in seven departments. Paul K. Whelton, MD, MSc, is senior vice president for the health sciences.

The School of Medicine and the School of Public Health hold the nation's largest MD/MPH degree program. Students at the School of Public Health and Tropical Medi-

cine also earn degrees in health systems management, epidemiology, tropical medicine, environmental health sciences, international health, community health sciences, biostatistics, and occupational safety and health.

The Tulane Regional Primate Research Center is the largest and the first of eight federally funded primate centers in the country. Located on the north shore of Lake Pontchartrain near Covington, the center focuses on infectious diseases caused by viruses, bacteria, and parasites, with a particular emphasis on the study of HIV infection and AIDS.

LOOKING TO THE FUTURE

Heading into the 21st century, Tulane University Health Sciences Center has implemented a multimillion-dollar strategic plan that will attract the best faculty, researchers, and students. The plan also includes centers for aging and chronic diseases such as hypertension, as well as expanding locations.

"We're thinking broadly," says Whelton. "We're thinking strategically. Where do we serve the community best? What is our fundamental vision of where we want to be 20 to 30 years from now?" ●

F OR MORE THAN 80 YEARS, DELGADO COMMUNITY COLLEGE HAS provided educational opportunities to the Greater New Orleans community. The largest and oldest two-year college in Louisiana, Delgado plays a vital role in the state's economic development by offering high-quality, cutting-edge career education at an affordable cost. ●●● Delgado opened its doors in 1921, a

realization of the vision of Isaac Delgado, a New Orleans businessman who saw the need for an institution for technical education. From these beginnings, Delgado has evolved into one of the largest providers of skilled, entry-level workers in Louisiana. Today, Delgado ranks 82nd in the nation out of 1,200 community and technical colleges in the number of associate degrees conferred, and 20th in the nation in the number of associate degrees conferred to African-Americans.

Most of Delgado's 50 associate degree programs and 22 certificate programs are career oriented and lead directly to employment, while others prepare students for transfer to four-year institutions. These academic programs are offered through eight programs of study: Arts and Humanities, Business Studies, Science and Mathematics, Communication, Nursing, Allied Health, Technology, and Occupational Studies.

Delgado also has a myriad of educational programs that have received national recognition for success in preparing students for the workforce. These programs include the Charity School of Nursing, Funeral Service Education, Radiological Technology, Medical Laboratory Technician, and Culinary Arts.

PREPARING STUDENTS FOR TOMORROW'S JOBS

D elgado is constantly working with local employers to develop new programs and update existing programs to better prepare students for both present and future jobs. Some of the current workforce development programs under way include the Incumbent Worker Program, which provides retraining to current workers and receives funding through the Louisiana Department of Labor; welfare-to-work training; and the concurrent Enrollment and Tech Prep Rising Star programs, which prepare high-school students for high-tech careers.

"Delgado is particularly strong at putting well-prepared graduates in the workforce," says J. Terence Kelly, chancellor. "We are responsive to the educational needs of the economy, and we help create jobs for local residents."

A BENEFIT TO THE COMMUNITY

I n addition to its original location, based in the heart of New Orleans, Delgado has extended its reach to include a total of four campuses across the metropolitan area. As a comprehensive community college, Delgado makes career education accessible for students from diverse racial, religious, economic, and cultural backgrounds. With enrollment of more than 20,000 students and a body of more than 100,000 alumni, Delgado provides its students with education that works. Students come to Delgado from every parish in Louisiana and from more than 30 states and 25 foreign countries.

Delgado does far more for the community than just train workers. By providing skilled labor, the college helps attract and retain high-paying jobs in Louisiana. In addition, total expenditures by Delgado for the fiscal year 1999-

2000 were some $60 million, resulting in more than $145 million in economic impact through reciprocal spending in the New Orleans-area economy.

FURTHERING STUDENTS' SUCCESS

I n addition to its educational programs, Delgado offers students a variety of support services to further their success. These include tutoring, computer labs, composition and math labs, career counseling, comprehensive testing, transfer planning, financial assistance, and student employment services. Delgado's libraries offer more than 100,000 books, a large selection of periodicals, and an array of on-line research services. Students can also participate in more than 40 clubs and organizations; the *Dolphin* student newspaper; student government; and many educational, social, and cultural events.

Since its inception, Delgado Community College has paved the way for a well-trained workforce to meet the changing needs of the local economy. Heading toward its centennial, Delgado continues its tradition of improving the lives of all citizens at all economic levels through quality, affordable education. ●

LAROCCA HALL, BUILT IN 1999 TO SERVE MORE THAN 2,000 STUDENTS ENROLLED AT THE WEST BANK CAMPUS, WAS NAMED IN HONOR OF HENRY ANDREW LAROCCA, A PHYSICIAN WHO WAS DEVOTED TO THE WELL-BEING OF WEST BANK CITIZENS. IT HOUSES 15 MULTIPURPOSE CLASSROOMS, A STATE-OF-THE-ART COMPUTER CLASSROOM, A STUDENT SERVICES AREA, THE PROVOST'S OFFICE, AND FACULTY OFFICES. THE BUILDING ALSO HAS A MULTIFUNCTIONAL, TIERED LECTURE HALL EQUIPPED WITH A VARIETY OF AUDIO-VISUAL CAPABILITIES, INCLUDING ON-LINE TELECONFERENCING (TOP).

DELGADO'S BUSINESS PROGRAMS EDUCATE THOUSANDS OF PEOPLE EACH YEAR FOR JOBS IN SOME OF THE FASTEST GROWING INDUSTRIES. STUDENTS HAVE ACCESS TO THE LATEST COMPUTER EQUIPMENT AND SOFTWARE FOR HANDS-ON TRAINING IN ACCOUNTING, BUSINESS ADMINISTRATION, COMPUTER INFORMATION TECHNOLOGY, LEGAL SECRETARY, AND ACCOUNTING (BOTTOM).

ROM SEAFOOD GUMBO TO JAMBALAYA, FOOD LOVERS WORLDWIDE savor the Cajun and Creole cuisine of New Orleans and southern Louisiana. An ingredient found in most Louisiana recipes is a dash of Tabasco® pepper sauce—a mix of aged pepper mash, vinegar, and salt—that has created a brand name as distinctive as its flavor. ●●● Producing some 500,000 bottles a day and dis-

tributing to more than 100 countries and territories, McIlhenny Company, located near New Orleans on Avery Island, has captured the world with its famous Tabasco pepper sauce. The military, world leaders, and even astronauts have been known to harbor a bottle of the potent pepper sauce to add spice to their meals.

"Following the traditions of New Orleans jazz and Cajun-Creole cuisine, Tabasco sauce is probably the single best-known

product by name from south Louisiana," says Paul C.P. McIlhenny, president and CEO. "And it's not just associated with Avery Island— it's Avery Island and New Orleans, because we have strong family relationships in both places."

SEASONED HISTORY

In 1841, Edmund McIlhenny moved from Hagerstown, Maryland, to New Orleans, where he became an agent for the Bank of Louisiana. By 1857, McIlhenny had

become an independent banker, owning five branch banks located throughout south and central Louisiana. In June 1859, he married Mary Eliza Avery, whose family owned a sugar plantation on Avery Island, then called Petite Anse Island after the bayou that partly encircles it. When the Civil War broke out in 1861, the Averys and McIlhennys sought refuge there. After discovering Avery Island's rock salt deposit, they oversaw the mining operation.

Upon the Union's invasion of Avery Island in 1863, the two families fled to east and central Texas. While in exile, McIlhenny worked as a civilian employee of the Confederate army. At the war's end, the families returned to Avery Island to recover the sugarcane fields and reorganize the salt-mining business.

Louisiana's banking industry was stifled by Reconstruction, so McIlhenny began experimenting with making pepper sauce, hitting upon a formula that called for crushing the reddest, ripest peppers; stirring in some Avery Island salt; and aging the concoction for at least 30 days. He then added French white wine vinegar and aged the mixture for at least another 30 days, hand stirring it to blend the flavors. After straining the mixture, McIlhenny transferred it to small, cologne-type bottles, which he corked and sealed in green wax. A metal sprinkler device was attached to the side of each bottle, to be fitted on the top of the bottle by the consumer after purchase.

After the sauce became popular with family and friends, McIlhenny decided to market it, growing his first commercial crop in 1868. He shipped 658 bottles at a dollar apiece to grocers in 1869 along the gulf coast and New Orleans. Consumers liked the fiery concoction, and McIlhenny secured a patent in 1870. E.C. Hazard and Company of New York City, a major food distributor,

CLOCKWISE FROM TOP LEFT: EDMUND MCILHENNY INVENTED TABASCO SAUCE IN THE LATE 1860S.

ONLY THE REDDEST, RIPEST PEPPERS ARE PICKED TO CREATE TABASCO SAUCE.

THE FIRST TABASCO FACTORY— KNOWN AS THE LABORATORY— OPERATED FROM 1868 TO 1905. IT WAS RECENTLY EXCAVATED BY AN ARCHAEOLOGICAL TEAM, YIELDING MANY SIGNIFICANT FINDINGS.

helped him introduce Tabasco sauce to major markets across the country. Soon, McIlhenny was exporting it internationally.

When Edmund McIlhenny died in 1890, his eldest son, John, took over the business with his mother's assistance. After John McIlhenny resigned in 1898 to join Theodore Roosevelt's Rough Riders cavalry regiment during the Spanish-American War, his brother Edward "Ned" McIlhenny presided over the company for some 51 years.

Ned McIlhenny, a visionary conservationist, established Jungle Gardens, an extension of Bird City, on Avery Island, which helped halt a threatened extinction of the egrets. When Ned died in 1949, Walter Stauffer McIlhenny, Edmund McIlhenny's grandson, was soon joined by Edward McIlhenny Simmons, Edmund McIlhenny's great-grandson, in running the business. And in 1967, a second great-grandson, Paul C.P. McIlhenny, president and CEO, joined the team.

A Growing Legacy

Although the original laboratory where McIlhenny invented his famous sauce was torn down around 1925, the building's remains were excavated in summer 2000 and 2001. A second plant was built in 1905, and a mod-ernized Tabasco plant at Avery Island has been in production since 1980.

Until the late 1960s, all of McIlhenny Company's peppers were grown on Avery Island. Now most of the pepper crop is grown in Latin American countries. Each picker uses a stick painted a bright, crimson red—called *le petit bâton rouge*—to determine if the peppers are ripe. Immediately after picking, the peppers are mashed with Avery Island salt and put in oak barrels to begin the three-year aging process in a warehouse on Avery Island. Strong vinegar is later added to the drained mash.

In the 1990s, McIlhenny Company—along with its original Tabasco pepper sauce—introduced a line of new sauces that include Tabasco green pepper sauce, Tabasco garlic pepper sauce, and Tabasco habanero pepper sauce. "Our future plans are to expand the Tabasco brand family of flavors and to consider the introduction of other Tabasco-branded condiments, such as steak sauce and mayonnaise," Paul C.P. McIlhenny says.

Each year, Avery Island welcomes approximately 100,000 guests to the Visitors Center and Tabasco Country Store, Jungle Gardens, and Bird City. McIlhenny Company has also opened other Tabasco Country Store branches in New Orleans, San Antonio, and Kemah, Texas. In 1996, the company launched the Tabasco PepperFest® Web site at www.TABASCO.com.

Rooted in the New Orleans area and steeped in flavorful tradition, McIlhenny Company is sure to prosper for generations to come. ●

TABASCO PEPPER MASH IS AGED FOR THREE YEARS IN WHITE OAK BARRELS. THIS MIXTURE IS LATER COMBINED WITH VINEGAR TO CREATE TABASCO PEPPER SAUCE (TOP LEFT).

ALTHOUGH TABASCO SAUCE IS SOLD IN VARIOUS SIZES, THE SHAPE OF THE BOTTLE HAS CHANGED LITTLE SINCE THE PRODUCT WAS FIRST SOLD COMMERCIALLY IN THE 1860s (TOP AND BOTTOM RIGHT).

WHITNEY NATIONAL BANK, THE OLDEST CONTINUOUSLY OPERATING bank in New Orleans, is a banking leader in the gulf area. Since the bank first opened in 1883, it has never closed its doors to customers, remaining open even during the Great Depression. ●●● The company has seen tremendous growth in recent years as it has expanded both in New Orleans and across the gulf area.

Businesses and consumers have been attracted both by the Whitney's tradition of relationship banking and by the value and convenience the bank offers.

People often remark that the Whitney feels like family. That's because the bank was founded by a family who remained active in the company for many years. Marie Louise Whitney and two of her sons—George and Charles—founded the bank, along with other prominent New Orleanians in 1883. The last Whitney to work at the bank was George Whitney's grandson, Morgan L. Whitney, who died in 1989.

COMMITTED TO NEW ORLEANS

The Whitney is one of the largest companies headquartered in New Orleans, and the bank has expanded both its New Orleans branch network and its staff over the past decade. The bank has built new branches in the city and surrounding parishes. A major investment is the Whitney Operations Center, which attracts talented technology professionals to the area.

Because of its commitment to the city, the bank provides resources and leadership to a diverse array of organizations. Whitney bankers work with United Way, the chamber of commerce, and many educational, cultural, and arts groups. The Whitney also works with housing organizations, striving to keep homes affordable for low- to moderate-income families. Annually, the bank fields a team to fix up a house for an elderly home owner. This effort helps keep people in their homes and preserves the city's unique architectural heritage.

GROWING WITH ITS CUSTOMERS

The Whitney has a unique franchise. The bank has chosen to follow its customers across the gulf area, rather than expanding to cover all of Louisiana. The bank noticed that many of its business customers had offices in Florida, Alabama, Mississippi, and Texas. Also, many New Orleanians travel across the gulf area along I-10. Following its customers, the bank expanded across southern Louisiana into Lafayette, then Baton Rouge, Morgan City, Houma, Thibodaux, and Lake Charles. The Whitney was the first Louisiana bank to enter Alabama. This move was followed by acquisitions in the Florida panhandle, Mississippi, and Houston.

Just as the bank has grown geographically to meet its customers' needs, so too has the product offering grown. For example, building on its long history of international banking, the Whitney has expanded its services in Central and South America. Traditionally, many residents of these regions have looked to New Orleans for financial and other services.

The Whitney has also experienced strong growth in its investments and trust business. A growing

JONATHAN POSTAL

THE WHITNEY NATIONAL BANK CLOCK IS A SYMBOL OF THE BANK'S HERITAGE. SINCE 1926, THE CLOCK HAS REPRESENTED THE WHITNEY AND ITS RICH HISTORY AND TRADITION.

PIERCE MOOR AND HER DAUGHTER ALEXIS BOUGHT THEIR FIRST HOME WITH THE HELP OF THE WHITNEY.

number of individuals have turned to the Whitney for professional investment management. Investors also use Whitney Securities for brokerage services.

The Whitney's traditional strength has always been its business services. An increasing number of New Orleans companies bank with the Whitney because they want local bankers who make decisions. New services such as on-line cash management through whitneybank.com are also important to the bank's customers.

The Whitney's consumer customer base is also growing. The company has added unique services such as Whitney SELECT, a relationship banking package, and Check & Save for value-oriented customers. Convenience is also important to consumers, and the company now offers on-line banking, an expanded call center, and many more ATMs around the city.

LEADERSHIP IN COMMUNITY BANKING

As the Whitney National Bank expands across the gulf area, the company combines its traditional banking strengths with contemporary ideas to meet the

rapidly changing needs of its customers. The Whitney still believes that banking is a people business, and being the best in community banking is the core of all of its activities. With this dedication to service, the Whitney will remain a cornerstone of the community and will continue to invest in New Orleans for generations to come. ●

MANY LOCAL BUSINESSPEOPLE HAVE BENEFITED FROM THE WHITNEY'S SERVICES, INCLUDING J.L. HOWARD (LEFT) AND DAVID ROBIEBEAUX, OWNERS OF SEAFOOD INTERNATIONAL IN BAYOU LABATRE, ALABAMA.

A TRADITION OF QUALITY SERVICE PROVIDED SINCE 1916 HAS LED Latter & Blum Inc./Realtors to the forefront of the real estate business in New Orleans and the Gulf South covering Louisiana and Mississippi. Throughout the firm's history, it has helped shape New Orleans' dynamic economy, while respecting its rich heritage—a balanced approach that has made Latter & Blum itself a part of the city's past, present, and dynamic future.

FOUNDING A FUTURE LEADER

In 1916, two young entrepreneurs, Harry Latter and Joseph Blum, formed a partnership that has flourished to become one of the largest and most successful real estate companies in the Gulf South. Latter arrived in New Orleans in 1908, bearing a brief letter of reference: "Harry Latter is a bright and willing lad and is sure to give satisfaction. He is leaving London." Latter's natural gifts for the real estate business, enhanced by his love and enthusiasm for his adopted city, were a perfect complement to the attributes of Joseph Blum, a quiet, thoughtful man who had never experienced the slightest doubt about the future of New Orleans.

In Latter & Blum's earliest years, its agents—who served both commercial and residential clients—handled all real estate transactions from a single, central location. Because the city's suburbs had not yet been developed, a large part of the business took place in the city, and the company handled primarily commercial real estate. During this period, the name Latter & Blum became synonymous with the incredible historical growth and development of the New Orleans region.

Latter & Blum's leadership responded to the growth and development of the city, and to the corresponding needs of its people for more specialized service, by adapting and expanding the company's operations. This expansion led to Latter & Blum's position as a market leader in the real estate industry, including services to clients needing homes, commercial and industrial properties, leasing, shopping centers, high-rise buildings, insurance, mortgages, and more. With its extensive background and expertise, Latter & Blum is positioned to handle both individual and large corporate clients.

BRANCHING OUT

In the early 1980s, as regional industries began to experience production slumps resulting from decreased oil production, Latter & Blum decided for the first time to attain leadership outside of the founders' families. Robert W. Merrick, a nationally respected appraiser, assumed ownership of Latter & Blum in 1986 and, within a few short years, grew the firm to its current regional presence as a dominant real estate firm in the Gulf South. Latter & Blum grew through internal growth, as well as through numerous large and small strategic acquisitions of quality real estate firms in the region.

Latter & Blum's growth has been constant in the years since, including the acquisition of more than 19 companies; the development of a large property management division in 1988; and the formation of Latter & Blum Insurance Services in 1991, Latter & Blum Network in 1998, and Essential Mortgage Company in 1999.

Latter & Blum has grown its nationally recognized relocation division to its current status as one of the largest organized relocation

ROBERT W. MERRICK SERVES AS CHAIRMAN AND CEO OF LATTER & BLUM INC./REALTORS (TOP).

IN LATTER & BLUM'S EARLIEST YEARS, ITS AGENTS—WHO SERVED BOTH COMMERCIAL AND RESIDENTIAL CLIENTS—HANDLED ALL REAL ESTATE TRANSACTIONS FROM A SINGLE, CENTRAL LOCATION (BOTTOM).

services in the Gulf South by handling more incoming corporate transferees than any other firm in the region. In 2001, Latter & Blum was recognized by RELO, the premier relocation network in the nation, as the top relocation broker in its category nationwide.

Latter & Blum expanded the company's operation into Baton Rouge when it opened two offices there in 1991, and bought C.J. Brown Realtors when owners of that well-established company, founded in 1917, decided to sell. The firm also expanded into the newly energized economy of the Mississippi gulf coast area, where three offices were opened in 1993. With these acquisitions and expansions, Latter & Blum became one of the nation's largest independent real estate companies. The company now encompasses more than 23 offices, and is ranked as the 21st-largest independent real estate company in America.

GIVING BACK TO THE COMMUNITY

With its own dynamic growth paralleling that of the New Orleans region, Latter & Blum continues to lead the way in business and community success in the Crescent City. Extending far beyond the realm of business, the company's contributions include its status as a good neighbor to the New Orleans area, where it has played a major

role in many projects and programs to improve the quality of life for all.

Latter & Blum's leaders have continued to support community endeavors of all types, including a donation to the city of the Latter family home for use as a public library, support of local schools, college scholarships offered to children of Latter & Blum employees, and continual support of such charitable organizations as United Way. Merrick, chairman and CEO, recently donated funds to the University of New Orleans College of Business to establish the Merrick Chair in Real Estate Finance.

Although Merrick has accomplished milestones as owner of Latter & Blum, he gives much credit to other key leaders of the company. Those include Arthur Sterbcow, president; Patrick J. Egan, executive vice president and director of the appraisal division; Robert C. Penick, vice president, treasurer, and CFO; Joseph S. Pappalardo, vice president and secretary, as well as serving as president of Latter & Blum Property Management, Inc.; and Richard P. Stone, vice president and director of the commercial division.

"At Latter & Blum Inc./Realtors and C.J. Brown Realtors, we are interested in being good neighbors, as well as in serving all of the community's real estate, property management, commercial, appraisal, mortgage, and insurance needs," Merrick says. "We take pride in our community, and in the 85-year family tradition that helped lay the groundwork that allowed our companies to flourish into the largest and most successful real estate company in the Gulf South." ●

WHEN JOSEPH MERRICK JONES FIRST OPENED THE DOORS TO HIS law practice in New Orleans on May 1, 1937, he hired only two associates. More than 60 years later, Jones, Walker, Waechter, Poitevent, Carrère & Denègre, L.L.P. is one of the largest law firms in the Gulf South region and the largest in Louisiana. ●●● Heading into the 21st century, Jones Walker—with more than

200 lawyers in offices in New Orleans, Baton Rouge, and Lafayette, Louisiana; Miami, Houston, and Washington, D.C.—counsels business leaders both at home and abroad. The firm's success and growth are credited to its ability to adapt to modern times, while still maintaining an entrepreneurial spirit.

JONES, WALKER, WAECHTER, POITEVENT, CARRÈRE & DENÈGRE, L.L.P., HEADQUARTERED IN NEW ORLEANS SINCE 1937, IS ONE OF THE FASTEST GROWING LAW FIRMS IN THE GULF SOUTH.

LOUISIANA LEADER IN EMERGING TECHNOLOGIES

Reflecting the diversity of Louisiana, Jones Walker embraces a wide variety of federal, state, and local law matters. From financial institutions to worldwide insurers, Jones Walker handles matters of regional, national, and international scope. The firm also views the representation of smaller businesses as equally important to the practice. Jones Walker strives to balance the traditional one-on-one relationship of attorney and client with the demands of today's increasingly complex legal problems, which often require the attention of a team of attorneys.

Jones Walker regularly serves as lead counsel in high-profile intellectual property litigation related to software and music piracy. The firm has an active and growing patent practice, as well as a telecommunications practice group that represents several of the largest providers of voice and data transmission services in the country. Jones Walker's attorneys assist these and other clients with Louisiana regulatory matters, antitrust litigation, corporate securities, and finance matters, as well as with mergers and acquisitions across the country.

IN THE INTERNATIONAL ARENA

Jones Walker's skills stretch far beyond the borders of Louisiana. The firm has assisted clients in closing more than $3 billion in cross-

border transactions since 1997, and provides advice on international business matters daily to clients operating overseas. Jones Walker's maritime practice, one of the world's largest, takes its focus to ports of call around the globe.

In recent years, Jones Walker has handled transactions on six continents. The firm's transactional international practice involves the representation of both American clients doing business abroad and foreign clients conducting, or desiring to conduct, business in the United States.

Jones Walker's attorneys have assisted clients in joint ventures, acquisitions of foreign and domestic entities, asset purchases, transportation and distributions arrangements, international construction contracts and subcontracts, and other real estate transactions. Such projects frequently involve an intersectional team of attorneys with expertise in international arbitration, as well as in litigation, tax, environmental, and corporate matters.

WINNING TEAM ENVIRONMENT

Throughout the years, Jones Walker's continued growth has enabled the firm to better serve the needs of its clients, while still maintaining the highest standards of legal service. By building strong, personal relationships with clients, the firm creates a working team environment that is focused on getting the best results in the most efficient manner.

In addition, numerous Jones Walker employees volunteer for various nonprofit organizations. Jones, Walker, Waechter, Poitevent, Carrère & Denègre, L.L.P.'s importance to the New Orleans community cannot be credited to any one partner or group of partners. The efforts of all of the partners throughout the years have made Jones Walker the success it is today. ●

WITH HUMBLE BEGINNINGS AS A SMALL BARGE REPAIR OUTFIT ON the Mississippi River in the late 1930s, Northrop Grumman Ship Systems' Avondale Operations in New Orleans has evolved into one of the most diversified shipyards in the United States. ●●● Northrop Grumman Ship Systems is headquartered in Pascagoula, and includes the Avondale Operations

in New Orleans, as well as the Ingalls Operations and the Full-Service Center, both located in Pascagoula. Ship Systems, which currently employs some 17,000 shipbuilding professionals, primarily in Louisiana and Mississippi, is one of the nation's leading companies for the design, engineering, construction, and life-cycle support of major surface ships for the U.S. Navy, the U.S. Coast Guard, and international navies, as well as for commercial vessels of all types.

"We're bigger, better, and stronger as a result of becoming part of Northrop Grumman and its Ship Systems sector," says Edward L. Winter, director of communications for Northrop Grumman Ship Systems' Avondale Operations. "As a result, we are well positioned and even more capable of being successful. It's an exciting time for Avondale."

MORE THAN 60 YEARS OF SHIPBUILDING EXCELLENCE

In 1937, Avondale founders James G. Viavant, Harry Koch, and Perry N. Ellis hired a small skiff to take them a few miles up the Mississippi River from New Orleans. The men knew that a marine ways could be created from the railroad-ferry crossing that was left obsolete with the opening of the Huey P. Long Bridge, so they took over a three-year lease from Southport Petroleum Company. In January, Viavant, Koch, and Ellis formed a barge construction and repair company called Avondale Marine Ways, Inc., which was formally chartered and incorporated in 1938.

The founders sought the services of engineer J.H. Bull to help construct the marine ways, and he soon joined the company as a partner. The four partners bought the 35-acre property from the Texas

and New Orleans Railroad in 1940, opening its doors to shipbuilding. During World War II, Avondale Marine Ways was awarded a contract by the U.S. Maritime Commission for oceangoing tugboats, which started the company's long involvement with federal government contracts.

The little barge repair outfit soon changed its name to Avondale Shipyards, Inc., and was purchased by the Ogden Corporation in 1959. In 1985, an employee stock ownership plan, consisting of seven industrial companies, formed Avondale Industries, Inc. In 1987, Avondale Industries sold six of the original seven companies. The shipyard remained as Avondale Industries, Inc. In 1999, Avondale joined the Litton Corporation as part of its Litton Ship Systems sector. In April 2001, Northrop Grumman acquired Litton, and Avondale became part of Northrop Grumman Ship Systems.

HEADING INTO THE 21ST CENTURY

Northrop Grumman Ship Systems' Avondale Operations enters the 21st century with leading-edge shipbuilding technology. Avondale's primary business is the design, construction, and life-cycle support of oceangoing ships, including amphibious assault and fleet support ships for the U.S. Navy, as well as icebreakers and cutters for the U.S. Coast Guard. Avondale's present commercial ship work includes double-hull crude carriers, and has also included product carriers, domestic cruise ships, LNG ships, and roll-on/roll-off ships. In addition, the diversified shipyards division has constructed oceangoing barges, complex chemical parcel carriers, offshore drilling rigs and drill ships, a hydroelectric power plant, and even an 800-bed floating detention facility for New York City.

In June 1998, the University of New Orleans-Avondale Maritime Technology Center of Excellence opened at Avondale. The center, the result of a unique partnership between the State of Louisiana, the University of New Orleans, and Avondale, offers the very latest in cutting-edge computer hardware and software design technology. The LPD 17 (landing platform dock) team is housed at the facility where it designed the revolutionary new ship. Avondale is currently constructing the first of an anticipated 12 LPD 17 Class amphibious assault ships for the U.S. Navy. Northrop Grumman Ship Systems' Avondale Operations employs approximately 6,000 workers in Louisiana and sponsors vocational training for several trades. ●

NORTHROP GRUMMAN SHIP SYSTEMS' AVONDALE OPERATIONS, WHICH SITS ON 265 ACRES IN NEW ORLEANS, HAS EVOLVED INTO ONE OF THE MOST DIVERSIFIED SHIPYARDS IN THE UNITED STATES.

BACK IN THE LATE 1930S, 19-YEAR-OLD PETER G. PAULI JR. began tinkering with broken bicycles in the backyard of his parents' New Orleans home. By 1938, his knack for repairing bicycles had turned into a full-fledged business, originally called Pauli's Bicycle Store, on Magazine Street. ●●● Located in the heart of historical uptown New Orleans, the shop soon out-

grew its humble beginnings, and Pauli expanded the store to display bicycles, accessories, and even lawn mowers. His brother Norman worked side by side with him, repairing lawn mowers, with Peter's wife, Bertha, helping to manage the store.

"When I was a kid, we lived above the store for years," recalls Sandra P. Gulley, Peter and Bertha's daughter, who is currently secretary, treasurer, and manager of the family business. "Business was doing so well, my father borrowed money from relatives and friends to open a store in Metairie. They all thought he was crazy. There was nothing out there."

But Peter Pauli knew there would be a demand for bicycles because new subdivisions were sprouting up in Metairie, a suburb of New Orleans. Incoming families would need bicycles for their children, as well as for themselves. The second Pauli's Bicycle Store opened in 1959, and during its first year, the store doubled the sales of the company.

Bertha Pauli continued to operate the Magazine Street store for about two years, and then the couple decided to relocate the entire business to the Metairie location. Because of the biking boom in the 1970s, Pauli's soon outgrew the Metairie building and the facil-

PAULI'S BICYCLE & FITNESS STORE IS TODAY LOCATED ON VETERANS BOULEVARD.

PETER G. PAULI JR. FOUNDED PAULI'S IN 1938.

PAULI'S ORIGINAL STORE WAS LOCATED ON MAGAZINE STREET.

ity was expanded to the present two-story, 10,000-square-foot store on Veterans Boulevard.

With strong family ties, Gulley followed in her father's footsteps in 1972. "It was one year after I had come home from college," she remembers. "Dad hooked me into answering the telephone, and then pushed me out onto the floor. I've been here ever since." Although Peter Pauli died in 1989, Gulley

and her mother, now the company's president, continue the family legacy.

PROVIDING SERVICE AND EXPERIENCE

Today's Pauli's Bicycle & Fitness Store carries bicycles for every member of the family, from 12-inch bicycles for toddlers to cruisers for grandparents. The display room features popular name-brand models, such as Schwinn, and specializes in bikes for the professional, as well as for the entire family. Offering a full line of exercise equipment, Pauli's was voted Best Bike Store by *Gambit Weekly* readers in 1999.

When a customer purchases a bicycle from Pauli's, the store's staff of experienced bike technicians assemble the bike free of charge. In addition, they service all bikes, regardless of where they were purchased.

Pauli's also believes in giving back to its community. For years, the store restored old bikes for underprivileged children in New Orleans' annual Toys for Tots campaign. The store's staff also volunteer their services for both the American Diabetes Tour de Cure and the Multiple Sclerosis Tour for Cure, as well as other cycling and fund-raising events.

"Like Dad used to say, 'Why hike? Ride a bike,'" remarks Gulley. "I'll carry on the family tradition at this location. I think bicycles will always be around." ●

FOR SOME 60 YEARS, OCHSNER CLINIC FOUNDATION HAS BEEN one of the most trusted names in health care. This medical complex has been the site to such miracles as the successful separation of Siamese twins, the first heart transplant in the South, and the implant of a pacemaker in the youngest patient on record—an infant only 12 hours old. Additionally, Alton

Ochsner, one of the original founders, was the first physician in the world to discover the link between cigarette smoking and lung cancer.

Four Tulane medical professors joined Ochsner to open the doors to Ochsner Clinic in New Orleans on January 2, 1942. Despite opposition from a medical community that held on to traditional practice views, the founders were determined to open a clinic where every diagnostic and therapeutic need of a patient could be filled in one building. Nineteen physicians were listed as staff members or consultants on the original staff roster. Today, more than 500 Ochsner physicians and surgeons practice in more than 70 medical specialties and subspecialties in more than 30 locations throughout southeast Louisiana.

In 1944, the partners of Ochsner Clinic established the Alton Ochsner Medical Foundation, a not-for-profit organization comprised of Ochsner Hospital and the foundation's Graduate Medical Education Division, Division of Philanthropy, and Research Institute. The hospital, a 427-bed, acute inpatient care facility, serves the needs of the New Orleans community, the Gulf South region, and a large international population. In addition, Ochsner is one of the largest non-university-based physician-training centers in the country. Established at its present location in 1954, the hospital has undergone several expansions and renovations, including its state-of-the-art Critical Care Tower in November 2000 and its Lieselotte Tansey Breast Center in June 2001.

Originally, the five founders of the physician-owned Ochsner Clinic intended to create a single organization, but Louisiana regulatory laws at the time prohibited physicians from owning a hospital. Nearly 60 years later, on August 31, 2001, Ochsner Clinic and the Alton Ochsner Medical Foundation became a single entity called Ochsner Clinic Foundation—achieving the initial vision of Dr. Alton Ochsner, Dr. Edgar Burns, Dr. Guy A. Caldwell, Dr. Francis E. LeJeune, and Dr. Curtis Tyrone.

CONTINUUM OF CARE

The hallmark of Ochsner care stems from a close collaboration between clinicians and

skilled scientists, which helps to bring medical discoveries from the laboratory to the bedside. Since 1995, *U.S. News & World Report* has consistently named Ochsner one of America's best hospitals. This rigorous annual assessment of all U.S. hospitals places Ochsner in the upper echelon in heart, gynecology, rheumatology, urology, and gastroenterology services. Additionally, for six consecutive years, Ochsner Hospital received the National Research Corporation's Consumer Choice Award for the New Orleans region.

For some 60 years, Ochsner Clinic Foundation has been widely recognized as a leader in research, patient care, and education. The commitment to these services continues today. ●

FOR SOME 60 YEARS, OCHSNER CLINIC FOUNDATION HAS BEEN ONE OF THE MOST TRUSTED NAMES IN HEALTH CARE.

WITH MORE THAN 1,200 ASSOCIATES AND 30 OFFICES SPANNING the New Orleans metropolitan area and southern Mississippi, Prudential Gardner, Realtors is the largest real estate company in the region, ranking in the top 1 percent of all real estate companies nationally. Prudential Gardner's services include the marketing, sales, financing, leasing, relocation, and property

management of residential, commercial, and industrial properties, achieving nearly $1.3 billion in annual sales volume.

The company was originally founded in New Orleans in 1943 as Gertrude Gardner, Realtors by Gertrude Gardner, a housewife and accomplished violinist originally from Tennessee. The family-run company grew steadily with the city, and on December 15, 2000, Gertrude Gardner, Realtors and Martha Ann Samuel, Realtors merged with Prudential Louisiana Properties and Prudential Bailey—the largest real estate company merger in Louisiana and Mississippi history—to form Prudential Gardner, Realtors.

THE COMPLETE REALTOR

Prudential Gardner has adapted to the changing times—dominated by more working couples with less free time—by becoming a one-stop shop to help its clients save time and money. "We changed our corporate mission statement from being the number one real estate services company to being the number one home lifestyle services company in the Gulf South," says Glenn

Gardner, president of operations. Some of these home lifestyle services include insurance, home warranties, home financing, home repairs, maintenance and renovations, and personal service coordinators to help both buyer and seller clients every step of the way—before, during, and after the completed sales transaction.

Technology is also helping Prudential Gardner grow. "Through the company's innovative Home-Link system, its personal service coordinators—who can be reached over the Internet or by phone—help clients with home inspections, moving companies, etc.," says Norris Songe, president of client services. To further its goal of customer satisfaction, Prudential Gardner maintains its own Web site at www. prudentialgardner.com, which features virtual tours of available properties, and a one-of-a-kind weekly television program on WDSU-TV, featuring many available homes. "We carry on that tradition of offering excellent service, and continue to improve on it because of new tools available to us through technology," says Barbara Blades, president of residential services. "Our goal in offering superior

ongoing service is to have a customer for life."

But it is personal service that truly makes this company a mainstay in the New Orleans real estate market. "One of the many reasons we are so successful is the golden rule that has been infused in this company by its earliest founder, Gertrude Gardner," Glenn Gardner says. "Gertrude always believed that if you treat customers honestly, fairly, and ethically—and work hard for their best interest—then you're bound to succeed."

This philosophy must be working because today, Prudential Gardner, Realtors is one of the highest-ranked companies in the nation. As a member of the Pinnacle Group and the Realty Alliance, Prudential Gardner was also the 2000 recipient of Prudential's top marketing award, the North American Performance Award for Outstanding Marketing Assistance. "Prudential Gardner plans to keep growing in size and performance," says Gardner. "We greatly appreciate all who have helped to make us the Gulf South's premier homegrown, locally owned, and internationally known real estate company." ●

THE PRUDENTIAL GARDNER, REALTORS TEAM INCLUDES (FROM LEFT) BARBARA BLADES, NORRIS SONGE, GLENN GARDNER, SHARON GARDNER, AND CHIP GARDNER, WHO ARE PICTURED HERE AT THE COMPANY'S 2000 MERGER.

THE WORLD TRADE CENTER (WTC) OF NEW ORLEANS IS A private, nonprofit organization of some 2,100 corporate and individual members. The organization has its roots in the International House, founded in 1943, and the International Trade Mart, founded in 1945, which merged in 1985. WTC New Orleans was the first of what, today, are more than 300 World Trade Center organizations—in more than 100 countries—that are members of the World Trade Centers Association. The association itself was founded in New Orleans in 1968.

WTC New Orleans' mission is to add wealth and jobs in Louisiana through international trade, port development, and allied activities. In line with these objectives, WTC has long been involved in conducting a wide range of trade promotion, educational, and legislative programs designed to enhance Louisiana's position in international trade, investment, transportation, banking, and other trade-related services, and to contribute to the state's overall economic development.

This wide variety of programs—many of which are detailed on the organization's Web site at www.wtc-no.org—includes training classes on exporting and importing, foreign language classes, seminars on doing business in various countries, international conferences and trade shows, international trade publications, and trade missions to other countries. In addition, over the years, countless dignitaries from throughout the world, as well as businessmen and business-women visiting Louisiana on trade missions or individually, have come to WTC New Orleans as honorees or speakers at a wide range of WTC programs.

A TRUE CENTER OF TRADE

WTC New Orleans also operates the 33-story World Trade Center Building on Canal Street on the riverfront, with tenants engaged in the full range of international trade activities. Amenities for building residents include a full-service U.S. post office; the Louisiana International Trade Center for import/export assistance; two conference rooms with conference-style seating capacities of 30 and 54, respectively; a gift shop and convenience store; a beauty/barber shop; a travel agency; and a valet dry cleaning service. The building is accessible 24 hours a day, and is in close proximity to a wide variety of hotels, the Ernest N. Morial Convention Center, the French Quarter, and the ferry landing.

The World Trade Center Building is easily reached via two major thoroughfares, Canal and Poydras streets, and offers direct access to Interstate 10. The building also makes available for its members and guests the Plimsoll Club, located on the 30th floor of the building overlooking the Mississippi River.

Through its programs, services, and facilities, World Trade Center of New Orleans serves as a catalyst in furthering Louisiana's trade with other countries and in bringing together international buyers and sellers to generate new business in the state. In recognition of its efforts, WTC New Orleans has received the President's E and E-Star awards for outstanding contributions to the expansion of U.S. exports. ●

THE WORLD TRADE CENTER CONDUCTS NUMEROUS SEMINARS, CONFERENCES, AND TRAINING PROGRAMS RELATED TO EXPORTING AND IMPORTING (LEFT).

THE 33-STORY WORLD TRADE CENTER BUILDING ON CANAL STREET ON THE RIVERFRONT IS HOME TO TENANTS ENGAGED IN THE FULL RANGE OF INTERNATIONAL TRADE ACTIVITIES (RIGHT).

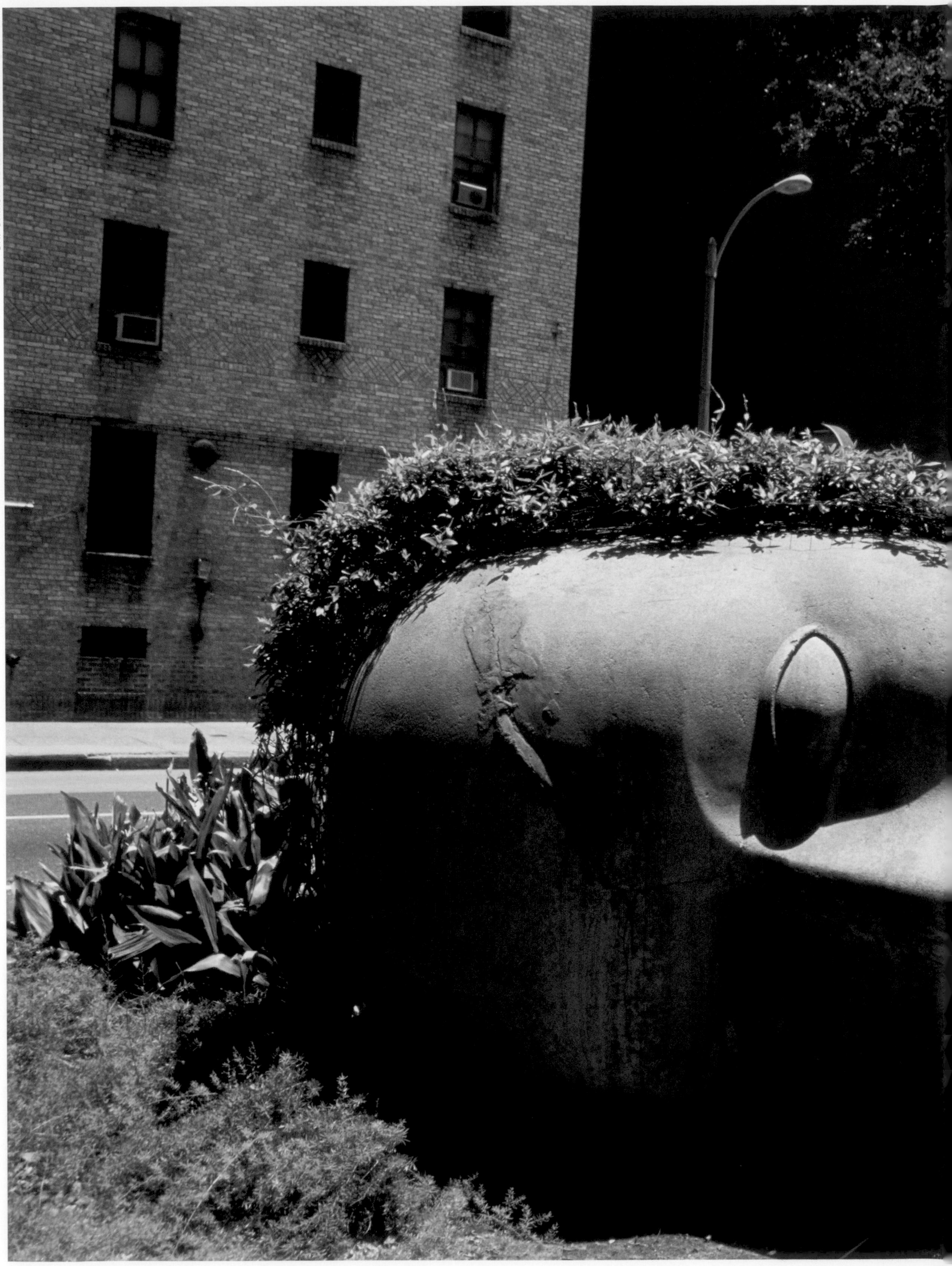

▲ © JONATHAN POSTAL / TOWERY PUBLISHING, INC.

1950-2002

1958
University of New Orleans

1969
Royal Sonesta Hotel and Chateau
    Sonesta Hotel

1974
McGlinchey Stafford, PLLC

1979
Taylor Energy Company

1986
Young Leadership Council

1989
RE/MAX New Orleans Properties

1994
Proud to Call It Home/
    New Orleans 24/7, Inc.

1995
Bally's Casino

1995
Tenet Hospitals of New Orleans

1997
Healthy New Orleans Partnership

1999
John A. Alario Sr. Event Center

LOCATED ON THE SITE OF A FORMER NAVAL AIR STATION AND overlooking the shore of Lake Pontchartrain, the University of New Orleans (UNO) opened its campus doors on September 5, 1958, to nearly 1,500 freshmen. UNO has since evolved into a comprehensive, urban university with nearly 16,000 undergraduate and graduate students, 800 faculty members, and

designation as America's Partnership University™. The university also promotes educational outreach through Metropolitan College, which offers credit and noncredit courses.

UNO, a member of the Louisiana State University System, was originally established as Louisiana State University in New Orleans, and was renamed the University of New Orleans in 1974. More than 50,000 degrees have been granted since the first graduating class in 1962, with nearly one-fourth of these at the master's or doctoral level.

Located five miles from downtown, the UNO Lakefront Campus includes a new Research and Technology Park adjacent to the main campus, and several satellite locations in the area. Today, UNO provides essential support for the economic, educational, and cultural development of the New Orleans community, and continues to distinguish itself in scholarship, research, and community service.

In recent years, UNO has been elected to the National Association of State Universities and Land-Grant Colleges and to the Association of American Colleges. UNO has also been ranked as one of Louisiana's top three Carnegie research universities; number one undergraduate naval architecture program in the United States; largest graduate school of education in the South; among the nation's top six film schools; number five environmental social science program in the nation; number five chemistry program in the Southeast; and number five political science program in the Southeast. The university's arena has been rated internationally as a top-10-grossing arena, seating some 5,000 to 10,000 people for 13 consecutive years. UNO also received the National Student Playwright award in both 1998 and 2000.

AMERICA'S PARTNERSHIP UNIVERSITY

As America's Partnership University enters the information age, both public and private partnerships will continue to be the dominant theme of Chancellor Gregory M. St. L. O'Brien's tenure. Most recently, the UNO Research and Technology Park opened with the Naval Information Technology Center as its anchor tenant and the Center for Energy Resources Management (CERM) as a new tenant, distinguishing Louisiana as a software hub. The UNO-Lee Circle Center, including the National D-Day Museum and the Roger H. Ogden Museum of Southern Art, promises to revitalize New Orleans' historic Lee Circle and Warehouse Arts District.

"UNO's partnerships are providing the technological base to help New Orleans fully participate in the information age," O'Brien says. "UNO is called America's Partnership University because it is so involved in building both the university and the community through partnerships that it is seen as a national model."

UNO's recently completed Partnerships 2000 capital campaign, which began in May 1996, raised $150 million. Partnerships with industry and government, such as the Naval Information Technology Center, the UNO/Avondale Maritime Technology Center of Excellence, and others have contributed an additional $360 million, creating 22 endowed chairs, 19 endowed professorships, more than $1 million in scholarships, and $15 million in programmatic and faculty support.

Other recent partnerships at the university include UNO's Gulf Coast Region Marine Technology Center, which participates in MARITECH, a national program to improve the U.S. shipbuilding industry's international competitiveness; and the UNO Audubon Institute Affiliation, a conservation program that studies endangered species.

Proving that partnerships aid in the realization of a university's potential, the University of New Orleans is a true asset to the community. ●

GREGORY M. ST. L. O'BRIEN SERVES AS CHANCELLOR OF THE UNIVERSITY OF NEW ORLEANS (UNO).

THE UNO LAKEFRONT CAMPUS IS LOCATED ON THE SOUTH SHORE OF BEAUTIFUL LAKE PONTCHARTRAIN IN NEW ORLEANS, ONLY MINUTES FROM THE CENTRAL BUSINESS DISTRICT AND THE WORLD-FAMOUS FRENCH QUARTER.

LOCATED ON BOURBON STREET IN THE HEART OF THE HISTORIC French Quarter, the Royal Sonesta Hotel New Orleans is a model of old-world charm. With a pink marble lobby glittering with chandeliers, wrought-iron balconies, and arched windows overlooking the garden courtyard, the Royal Sonesta Hotel has long been a top choice for foreign dignitaries, politicians, celebrities, and tourists visiting the Crescent City.

"We are very proud that we have provided our customers with a true French Quarter experience for more than 30 years," says Hans U. Wandfluh, president and general manager. "Our hotels are an oasis of quiet elegance in the midst of the diversified activities of the French Quarter."

The site of the four-star grand hotel, which was actually cobbled together from various pieces of property facing Bourbon, Bienville, Royal, and Conti streets, has historical roots dating back to 1721, when the French military engineer Adrien de Pauger first laid out the city of New Orleans. In 1967, following the demolition of the buildings on these properties, construction began with plans that paid special attention to the architectural integrity of the French Quarter.

Since the $16 million, landmark hotel opened its doors in 1969, the Royal Sonesta has served as a breathtaking centerpiece to a multitude of renowned Cajun and Creole restaurants, jazz clubs, and antique shops. Welcoming guests through its beveled glass doors, the hotel has 500 European-style guest rooms, which include 35 suites and a privately accessed floor with a personal concierge. After a day of sightseeing, guests can relax by the pool or in the tropical courtyard.

The Royal Sonesta offers some of the best dining and entertainment experiences inside its own doors. While Begue's Restaurant offers fine dining, the Desire Oyster Bar & Bistro offers a more casual menu with lively streetside dining. At the Mystick Den and Can Can Jazz Café, guests can enjoy nightly entertainment. And Le Booze is the perfect place to spy on the local scene. In addition, the Royal Sonesta has 20 meeting rooms to host events, from a private dinner in the Bienville Suite to an executive business meeting in the elegant, 5,000-square-foot Grand Ballroom.

"We are committed to providing our customers with a quality hotel experience and excellent value for their expenditures," says Wandfluh, who has been with the Royal Sonesta for more than 20 years. "We are also committed to providing an excellent work environment to all employees."

CHATEAU SONESTA

The Chateau Sonesta Hotel, on Iberville Street in the French Quarter, opened its doors in 1995. The building, which dates back to the pre-Civil War era, was the former site of the renowned D.H. Holmes Department Store. The store's 1913 facade was restored to its original beauty, complete with the famous Holmes clock and a statue of Ignatius Reily, featured in *A Confederacy of Dunces,* John Kennedy Toole's Pulitzer Prize-winning novel.

The Chateau Sonesta has 251 spacious rooms with cathedral ceilings and three breathtaking courtyards. Other features include an outdoor pool, a fitness room, the restaurant La Chatelaine, the Red Fish Grill, the Clock Bar, and 10,000 square feet of meeting space. The hotel is the perfect place to bring families, offering movie rentals, video games, and a baby-sitting service. The Chateau Sonesta was voted a best family-friendly hotel by *Parents* magazine.

Both the Royal Sonesta Hotel and the Chateau Sonesta Hotel are owned by Sonesta International Hotels Corporation, which operates 17 upscale hotel and resorts worldwide, as well as two Nile cruisers. ●

BOTH THE ROYAL SONESTA HOTEL AND THE CHATEAU SONESTA HOTEL OFFER ELEGANT ACCOMMODATIONS IN THE HEART OF THE FRENCH QUARTER.

O N JANUARY 1, 1974, A HANDFUL OF ATTORNEYS ESTABLISHED A small law firm in office space in the heart of the central business district in New Orleans. Due to their dedication and commitment to their clients and community, the founding attorneys of McGlinchey Stafford, PLLC soon outgrew their modest beginnings, and made a decision that would positively change

the landscape of their historical city.

In fewer than 10 years, McGlinchey Stafford paved the way for the restoration of the practically abandoned warehouse district. While aiding numerous clients with its expert legal service, the law firm has transformed the community with historical renovations and philanthropic donations.

PIONEERS OF THE FAUBOURG-ST. MARY HISTORIC DISTRICT

McGlinchey Stafford first opened its office doors on the 43rd floor of the One Shell Square Building. When the firm outgrew the office space in 1979, McGlinchey Stafford considered relocating its practice to an area across from the central business district called the warehouse district, or Faubourg-St. Mary Historic District. The section of town was filled with abandoned, turn-of-the-century warehouses.

However, McGlinchey Stafford had the foresight to believe that a firm in the warehouse district would prosper, since the federal courthouses were a stone's throw

away. The firm forged a path across Poydras Street in 1979 and purchased the former Eli Lilly Pharmaceutical Building on Camp Street. Thus, McGlinchey Stafford spearheaded the restoration of the Faubourg-St. Mary Historic District, and paved the way for numerous other law firms and corporations to follow.

The old pharmaceutical building, completely renovated under the direction of architects Errol Barron and Michael Toups, opened its

McGlinchey Stafford, PLLC's restoration of two warehouses on Poydras and Magazine streets spearheaded the restoration of the Faubourg-St. Mary Historic District, and paved the way for numerous other law firms and corporations to follow.

doors on January 1, 1980. While the remodeled building offered room for additional attorneys and staff, the rapid growth that the firm experienced in the coming years sparked yet another major renovation project of a former antiques warehouse on Magazine Street.

McGlinchey Stafford's multi-million-dollar renovation, masterminded by Barron and Toups, demonstrated that historic buildings can be reconverted for contemporary use without destroying the 19th-century character of New Orleans' neighborhoods. The brick warehouse structure—an amalgam of three separate buildings unified by a brick exterior wall—was transformed into award-winning office space with such nontraditional law firm features as a circular library occupying three floors, a café serving breakfast and lunch daily, and conference rooms in towers spanning the four floors of the building. Although a fire in January 1984 postponed the grand opening, the doors to the new offices opened for business in September 1984. The renovation project received several awards, and served as an example for other companies to follow in the historical area.

SERVING CLIENTS' NEEDS

The McGlinchey Stafford law firm has a total staff of some 400 employees, with approximately 160 attorneys in seven offices in Louisiana, Mississippi, Texas, and Ohio. The full-service firm's practice areas include banking and consumer finance, products liability, labor and employment, business and general litigation, admiralty, and health care. The firm's attorneys are committed to acquiring in-depth knowledge of their clients' businesses, not only to achieve prompt, positive resolution of legal problems, but also to anticipate and prevent legal problems from developing in the first place.

Although its New Orleans office remains the headquarters for the firm, McGlinchey Stafford is committed to growth that satisfies the needs of its clients. Recently, the firm opened its Cleveland, Ohio, office to expand its capabilities in the area of consumer finance compliance and litigation.

GIVING BACK TO THE COMMUNITY

McGlinchey Stafford's attorneys remain dedicated to the community by serving on the boards of charities, schools, and civic organizations. The firm has been named a United Way Pacesetter for its annual fundraising campaigns. In addition, the McGlinchey Stafford Foundation was created to provide financial assistance to worthy organizations. Since 1991, the foundation has provided more than $1 million of support to charities, schools, human services, the arts, and other nonprofit organizations.

As McGlinchey Stafford, PLLC continues to expand, the home-based firm will always remain faithful and committed to the New Orleans community. ●

McGLINCHEY STAFFORD'S BRICK WAREHOUSE HEADQUARTERS—AN AMALGAM OF THREE SEPARATE BUILDINGS UNIFIED BY A BRICK EXTERIOR WALL—WAS TRANSFORMED INTO AWARD-WINNING OFFICE SPACE WITH SUCH NONTRADITIONAL LAW FIRM FEATURES AS A CIRCULAR LIBRARY OCCUPYING THREE FLOORS, A CAFÉ SERVING BREAKFAST AND LUNCH DAILY, AND CONFERENCE ROOMS IN TOWERS SPANNING THE FOUR FLOORS OF THE BUILDING.

DESCRIBED BY MANY AS A MAVERICK, PATRICK F. TAYLOR ESTABlished Taylor Energy Company, one of the largest oil companies—and the only independent oil company—operating in the federal waters off the shores of the United States in the Gulf of Mexico. Although Taylor has accomplished milestones in the oil industry, the self-made millionaire is best known as a

national role model and reformist in higher education for implementing the Taylor Plan across the United States.

Growing up in Beaumont, Taylor dreamed of becoming an oilman. Through hard work and academic achievement, he earned a scholarship to the prestigious Kinkaid Prep School in Houston. After graduating from Kinkaid, he had no funds to attend college. Taylor soon learned that Louisiana State University (LSU) was the only school in the region he could afford to attend, since the university did not charge tuition. Enrolling at LSU with a loan to pay for room and board, Taylor completed his degree in petroleum engineering in three and a half years.

Upon graduation, Taylor remained in Louisiana and worked for John Mecom Sr., an independent Houston oilman. Taylor and Mecom established Circle Bar Drilling Company, a shallow-water drilling firm. In 1979, the firm was sold, and Taylor formed his own exploration and production company, Taylor Energy Company, based in New Orleans.

Taylor is proud of his company's success. But his true passion lies with ensuring that tomorrow's generation has the opportunity to

obtain a college education. In 1988, Taylor challenged 183 students who had failed at least two times at Livingston Middle School in East New Orleans. He told them that if they took college preparatory courses and attained a B average, he would make sure they could attend college. Approximately half of these original Taylor Kids graduated from high school and half of these entered college.

After witnessing the enthusiasm of these students, Taylor began a quest at his own expense to enact legislation that would ensure that all qualified Louisiana children would have the opportunity to attend college—based on their ability to learn, not on their ability to pay. Thus, the Taylor Plan became his brainchild.

"The three factors that are most important are that the Taylor Plan provides kids in grades K to 12 with motivation, motivation, motivation. A properly motivated kid can get an adequate education in the poorest of schools, but an unmotivated kid cannot get an education in the best of schools," Taylor says.

By researching higher education in Louisiana, Taylor discovered that public four-year colleges and universities did not require entrance

standards, and nearly 70 percent of all students who enrolled were dropping out before completing a degree. He began to promote the idea that those colleges and universities should require entrance standards of at least a 20 ACT test score, a 2.5 grade point average, and completion of 17.5 credits of college-preparatory classes. In return, students who qualified—but who where members of lower- and middle-income families—could obtain a college education through state payment of fees. Through Taylor's determination, the Taylor Plan was passed by the Louisiana legislature and signed into law by Governor Charles Roemer in 1989. By 2001, Taylor's plan had been implemented in 18 more states. In 1997, the family income requirement was removed from the Taylor Plan, and the plan name was changed to Tuition Opportunity Program for Students (TOPS).

"It's a win-win situation for the universities because they are getting more and better qualified kids," Taylor says. "It's also a win-win situation for the students because they are not going to fail in college. They graduate in three to four times the number of the average kids." ●

CARROLL S. GREVEMBERG

CLOCKWISE FROM TOP RIGHT: PATRICK F. TAYLOR ESTABLISHED TAYLOR ENERGY COMPANY IN 1979.

TODAY, THE TAYLOR PLAN IS RAISING ACADEMIC STANDARDS IN 19 STATES.

TAYLOR'S DEDICATION TO EDUCATION BEGAN IN 1988 WITH THESE STUDENTS FROM LIVINGSTON MIDDLE SCHOOL.

CARROLL S. GREVEMBERG

YOU CAN GO TO COLLEGE.
It's not just a promise. It's the law.

IN 1989, MARY ANN CASEY-THERIOT, AFTER WORKING IN A conventional real estate office for several years, made a decision that would change the landscape of the real estate market in New Orleans forever. Although most local firms had come from family names associated with brokering real estate for decades, Casey-Theriot seized the opportunity and

bought a RE/MAX franchise. In 1973, RE/MAX International was founded on the premise that top real estate agents could share overhead and expenses while keeping 100 percent of their commissions. Today, RE/MAX has nearly 65,000 associates and 4,000 offices in 37 countries and continues to grow.

During the first year of its operation, Casey-Theriot moved RE/MAX New Orleans Properties' location from the midcity area to uptown New Orleans, and opened a second office in the Lakeview area. Although other real estate organizations, title companies, and lending institutions crowded that four-block, midcity stretch, Casey-Theriot staked a claim in the heart of the local real estate industry with her savvy and knowledge of the profession.

"I entered into real estate because my father and three brothers were general contractors," Casey-Theriot says. "I grew up reading blueprints on the dining room table and seeing homes built from the ground up. I came to appreciate the privilege of home ownership."

MARKET EXPANSION

Following Casey-Theriot's lead as the first RE/MAX franchise in New Orleans, other brokers soon recognized the opportunity, buying the RE/MAX concept and opening franchises in Jefferson and St. Tammany parishes. The RE/MAX stronghold and market share in the area expanded.

"Our agents average almost three times the number of transactions and dollar volume of traditional agents," Casey-Theriot states. "Typically, RE/MAX agents are full-time professionals who have joined RE/MAX in order to be in control of their own business and to earn more income."

GROWING THE BUSINESS

As Casey-Theriot's company grew, the need for expansion became apparent. In 1997, she took yet another risk by buying and completely renovating two turn-of-the-century buildings in the same area. Although she was selling real estate, raising two daughters, and managing two offices, Casey-Theriot rose to the task. "We were excited to be part of a historical restoration, and we even won the Golden Hammer Award, given by the city of New Orleans in 1998," she says. But more than just a historical landmark, the new facility is a state-of-the-art real estate office complete with a satellite hookup offering RE/MAX educational programming and a sophisticated computer network system.

Today, New Orleans' two RE/MAX offices are among the highest producers in the area, and the company had the top two agents in the state of Louisiana in 1999 and 2000. "We have had continuous growth, averaging 12 to 15 percent per year," Casey-Theriot says. "Most companies today grow in size by acquisitions. We, however, have grown by recruiting top agents and increasing sales volume."

With more than 40 agents at both locations and continuous market-share growth, Casey-Theriot is still leading the way in the real

estate industry. In 2000, the innovative businesswoman pioneered yet another hallmark on the local real estate landscape by partnering her offices with a title company and forming the Title Group, LLC.

A FAMILY ENDEAVOR

Casey-Theriot's older daughter, Sarah Ackerman, knows about her mother's triumphs in the real estate business firsthand, since she has been a licensed agent and her mother's assistant since 1996. Casey-Theriot hopes her younger daughter, Rachael Casey, will one day join the team.

"The real source of joy for me has been to see our ever expanding group of clients and the effect RE/MAX has had on them, as well as on me and my family, and on the lives and families of my many agents," Casey-Theriot says. RE/MAX New Orleans Properties is also involved in the Children's Miracle Network, helping to contribute to the $4.5 million raised by RE/MAX associates in 2000. "The funds raised locally go directly to the Children's Hospital of New Orleans here in the uptown area," Casey-Theriot says. "There is no reward greater than helping children. My vision is to continue to grow into an organization of top agents, and to increase our market share and presence in the community. We can go nowhere but up." ●

GREVY PHOTOGRAPHY

MARY ANN CASEY-THERIOT FOUNDED RE/MAX NEW ORLEANS PROPERTIES IN 1989.

IN THE SPRING OF 1986, SIX YOUNG NEW ORLEANIANS WHO HAD been working together on both sides of the mayoral campaign decided to continue their affiliation by tackling the social and economic problems facing the city. Feeling that New Orleans' existing civic organizations would not afford young adults opportunities for hands-on involvement in their community,

the six formed a new organization, the Young Leadership Council (YLC).

"The organization was founded with a little streak of rebellion," says John Hopper, executive director. "Like any smart businessperson, you don't go out and reinvent the wheel. But in 1986, there wasn't an organization doing what the founders of YLC envisioned."

Today, YLC has grown to more than 1,100 members, who volunteer more than 15,000 hours annually with 30 community projects. Although anyone may join, active voting members are between the ages of 21 and 42, and make up the majority of the organization's membership.

THE VISION OF YOUNG LEADERSHIP COUNCIL'S (YLC) NEWEST PROJECT, GREEN I-10, IS TO LANDSCAPE THE INTERSTATE FROM THE LOUIS ARMSTRONG NEW ORLEANS INTERNATIONAL AIRPORT TO THE MISSISSIPPI BORDER.

THE IMPACT OF YLC

Since its founding, YLC has made numerous contributions to the New Orleans community, including several hallmark accomplishments for which the organization will always be known. In 1987, YLC, through its Sports Vision Committee, conducted a study on the potential economic development of sports in the community. The study led to the creation of the Greater New Orleans Sports Foundation, which has contributed hundreds of millions of dollars to the local economy.

Other notable YLC projects include the 1991 lighting of the Crescent City Connection, the bridge joining New Orleans' east and west banks of the Mississippi River, and the Proud to Call It Home campaign, launched in 1994 as an intensive, multifaceted effort to improve residents' attitudes regarding New Orleans as a great place to live and work. The impact of the Proud to Call It Home initiative still reverberates through the dialogue of the city's citizens.

In 2000, YLC, along with the Arts Council of New Orleans, launched the Festival of Fins, the largest public art display ever to hit New Orleans. More than 200 four-foot-high fish sculptures were painted by local artists and displayed throughout the city. A charity auction at the end of the Festival of Fins event raised more than $550,000 and benefited 65 local nonprofit organizations. The vision of YLC's newest project, Green I-10, is to landscape the interstate from the Louis Armstrong New Orleans International Airport to the Mississippi border.

"Those are some of [YLC's] more highly visible public awareness projects," Hopper adds. "But, at the end of the day, YLC is about kids and education. That's the focus of the majority of our projects, and where the majority of our volunteers spend their time." YLC has a multitude of projects through which volunteers positively impact children's lives.

YLC'S NEIGHBORHOOD RENAISSANCE PARTNERSHIP IS COMMITTED TO REVITALIZING NEW ORLEANS' NEIGHBORHOODS. VOLUNTEERS PRESENT A FREE ANNUAL SEMINAR FOR PROSPECTIVE HOME BUYERS, AND WORK WITH HABITAT FOR HUMANITY AND CHRISTMAS IN OCTOBER TO RENOVATE, REBUILD, OR PRESERVE HOMES FOR NEEDY RESIDENTS.

CLOCKWISE FROM TOP:
REACH OUT AND READ VOLUN-
TEERS READ BOOKS TO AND PROVIDE
BOOKS FOR CHILDREN AT LOCAL
HOSPITALS.

IN 2000, YLC, ALONG WITH THE
ARTS COUNCIL OF NEW ORLEANS,
LAUNCHED THE FESTIVAL OF FINS.
MORE THAN 200 FOUR-FOOT-HIGH
FISH SCULPTURES WERE PAINTED
BY LOCAL ARTISTS AND DISPLAYED
THROUGHOUT THE CITY. A CHARITY
AUCTION AT THE END OF THE FESTI-
VAL EVENT RAISED SOME $550,000
AND BENEFITED 65 LOCAL NON-
PROFIT ORGANIZATIONS.

AT YLC'S SUMMER BAND CAMP,
PROJECT PRODIGY, MORE THAN
160 YOUTH RECEIVE QUALITY MUSIC
INSTRUCTION, LEARNING FROM AND
PERFORMING WITH LOCAL MUSICIANS
AT THE CAMP'S CLOSING RECITAL.

At YLC's summer band camp, Project Prodigy, more than 160 youth receive quality music instruction, learning from and performing with local musicians at the camp's closing recital. Through U Go Girl, preteen and teenage girls learn computer and Internet skills. Recreate New Orleans provides an outlet for community outreach to at-risk children in and around the B.W. Cooper Housing Development; its volunteers provide year-round basketball and arts and crafts activities for more than 200 children. Volunteers who are active with projects such as Meth-odist Home, Academy Angels, and Reach Out and Read serve as mentors, tutors, and friends to children in need.

Other YLC projects focus on New Orleans' neighborhoods, culture, and economic development. YLC's Neighborhood Renaissance Partnership is committed to revitalizing New Orleans' neighborhoods. Volunteers present a free annual seminar for prospective home buyers, and work with Habitat for Humanity and Christmas in October to renovate, rebuild, or preserve homes for needy residents. New Orleans' culture is preserved as well through YLC's Attending Arts, a project that supports and develops the arts in the community. YLC partners with the national Dress For Success program to provide suits and job training for women transitioning from welfare to work.

Young Leadership Council is always looking for the next opportunity to build a better New Orleans. YLC's volunteers continue to create new projects and service outlets for the young leaders of the community to tackle. The results of these projects give all New Orleans residents a reason to be Proud to Call It Home. ●

IN 1994, VOLUNTEERS FROM THE YOUNG LEADERSHIP COUNCIL initiated a campaign that became one of the longest-running image campaigns in the nation: New Orleans, Proud to Call It Home. ●●● While other cities have tried slogans that might have gained more international recognition, the Proud to Call It Home campaign aspired for local greatness with tremendous success. Its goal was to improve attitudes and teach local metro residents why New Orleans is such a great place to both live and work.

A NOTEWORTHY CITY

After nearly $1.5 million in contributions, along with original uses of the Proud to Call It Home slogan on bumper stickers, pins, hotel parking lot walls, billboards, and T-shirts, the program has developed many creative ways to say "I love New Orleans"—in English, French, Spanish, and Vietnamese—and continues to be tremendously effective in marketing the city's image.

The secret of the campaign is simple: low-cost, mass-market techniques to educate the city about its treasures, as well as the dissemination of information such as which hotels are on the world's top 10 list and which native chefs are considered among the world's best. In addition, New Orleans' port, numerous colleges and universities, world-famous music, low tax rate, and internationally

respected medical community add up to a city that is always noteworthy. The Proud to Call It Home campaign helps empower residents to say why they are invested in this community, and why they want others to join them.

Proud to Call It Home is the first image campaign in the city's history to have measured local attitudes and perceptions before and after its media and educational campaigns; the survey found a marked difference. In fact, the campaign was so successful that its famous cup and logo rank right up there with local icons such as K&B purple, crawfish at Jazzfest, and the Mardi Gras Mambo.

THE SUCCESS AND FUTURE OF NEW ORLEANS

Although it has taken literally tens of thousands of volunteers—especially those sporting Proud to Call It Home bumper stickers on their cars—to make this grassroots campaign a success, the idea is really the brainchild of three local marketing experts: Ti Martin, proprietor of Commander's Palace; Trudy Noles, vice president of Hibernia National Bank; and Karyn Noles, managing facilities director of Audubon Aquarium of the Americas.

In any celebration of New Orleans, its talent, and its resources, revelers should realize that the city itself reflects the spirit of the city's leaders. These enterprising men and women see a need and fill it, through organizations like the Young Leadership Council and New Orleans 24/7.

"Forward-thinking leaders and fresh ideas are critical to the success and future of the city," says Paulette Irons, a state senator and a Proud to Call It Home sponsor. "The vitality and vision of the leaders of New Orleans represent why residents are proud to call New Orleans home." ●

CLOCKWISE FROM TOP: PROUD TO CALL IT HOME USES A FACT-BASED APPROACH TO BUILD PRIDE IN NEW ORLEANS, OFTEN TOUTING THE LATEST CRIME STATISTICS, COMPARISONS BETWEEN NEW ORLEANS AND OTHER CITIES, AND INFORMATION ABOUT THE CITY'S HOME-BASED INDUSTRIES.

CIVIC LEADERS—NEW ORLEANS SAINTS PLAYERS, BUSINESS LEADERS, AND POLITICIANS—FROM ALL OVER NEW ORLEANS HAVE LINED UP TO DONATE THEIR TIME TO THE PROUD TO CALL IT HOME CAMPAIGN.

SENATOR PAULETTE IRONS IS A SPONSOR OF THE YOUNG LEADERSHIP COUNCIL AND NEW ORLEANS 24/7, INC.

New Orleans
Proud to call it home.

SINCE THE 1960S, ORLEANS PARISH HAS EXPERIENCED A consistent migration of residents leaving the city limits. From 1980 to 1990, some 75,000 residents moved out of New Orleans. Hoping to stem the tide of fleeing residents, a group of community activists banded together in 1999 to bring people back to the city. Jeanette Bell, Louise Martin, Harry McCall, Jim Pertuit, Camille Strachan, Jazz Washington, and Peggy Wilson made a 24-hour-a-day, seven-day-a-week commitment to restore the population of their city. Thus, New Orleans 24/7, Inc. was born.

New Orleans 24/7 is a non-profit organization that markets New Orleans as a prime residential destination, with the intent of increasing the city's population and building a stronger community. Eventually, the nonprofit organization, which received seed funding from Paulette Irons, state senator, hopes to spawn an inward migration of population to the city. This will create a new demand for residential opportunities in New Orleans, resulting in a broader tax base, improved neighborhoods, and increased sense of community, all contributing to a better city in which to live.

GETTING THE MESSAGE OUT

New Orleans 24/7 has two objectives: to reach residents of the New Orleans suburbs with a compelling message to return to the city and to reach heads of highly targeted nontraditional households visiting the city, such as retirees; empty nesters; single, young professionals; and artists.

New Orleans 24/7 projects its message through the use of targeted print and broadcast media, as well as with a carefully crafted public relations plan. This plan—explained in materials that tourists are encouraged to take home—reaches the tourist market in places frequently visited for information on local attractions. New Orleans 24/7's Web site—www.neworleans24-7.org—is also a vital part of the organization's target marketing. The Web site provides information on the area, and gathers and tracks information from reader feedback.

New Orleans 24/7 also hosts

special events to help locals and tourists gain awareness of all New Orleans has to offer. For example, New Orleans 24/7 and the Young Leadership Council's Proud to Call It Home Committee cosponsor DeTour New Orleans, an annual event held during Jazzfest. Neighborhood representatives guide Jazzfest visitors through neighborhoods they normally would not visit as tourists, and show them homes that are for sale. New Orleans 24/7 also sponsors continuing education programs for local Realtors to enable them not only to sell houses, but also the neighborhoods and the city.

Hoping to make recent transplants active members of the community, the semiannual Newest Orleanians' Breakfast welcomes new residents to New Orleans by providing an introduction to the mayor and other city officials, entertainment, and information on local nonprofit activities and volunteer opportunities. The breakfast, sponsored by New Orleans 24/7, is supported by an Economic Development Fund grant from the City of New Orleans, sponsorships, and in-kind donations.

"This type of organization underscores our commitment to home ownership," says Desiree Charbonnet, Orleans recorder of mortgages and New Orleans 24/7 board member. "We're a city of neighborhoods, and we're taking every step to preserve and strengthen these places we call home." ●

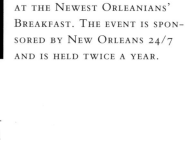

NEW ORLEANS 24/7 VOLUNTEER SUE DEASY WELCOMES NEW RESIDENTS AT THE NEWEST ORLEANIANS' BREAKFAST. THE EVENT IS SPONSORED BY NEW ORLEANS 24/7 AND IS HELD TWICE A YEAR.

JAZZFEST VISITORS VISIT AN IRISH CHANNEL ESTATE DURING THE DETOUR NEW ORLEANS, SPONSORED BY NEW ORLEANS 24/7 AND THE YOUNG LEADERSHIP COUNCIL.

Guests of the red, white, and blue riverboat known as *Belle of Orleans,* now dockside at Lake Pontchartrain, experience the thrill of gaming, the unique flavor of New Orleans cuisine, and the toe-tapping rhythm of live entertainment. Bally's Casino at South Shore Harbor in eastern New Orleans is the only riverboat casino still operating in New Orleans. ●●● "Our mission is to provide the ultimate entertainment experience to our guests through hospitality, service, and professionalism," says Mia Caldwell, marketing operations manager. "Our mission affords us the opportunity to continue to captivate this market and expand beyond."

Bally's Casino, owned and operated by Belle of Orleans, LLC, a subsidiary of Park Place Entertainment, opened its doors in 1995. The triple-deck riverboat casino spans two gaming levels for a total of 30,000 square feet. Located 15 minutes from the central business district and 10 miles from the historical French Quarter of New Orleans, the riverboat attracts more than 2 million patrons annually.

BALLY'S CASINO, A TRIPLE-DECK RIVERBOAT CASINO, SPANS TWO GAMING LEVELS FOR A TOTAL OF 30,000 SQUARE FEET.

VARIED ENTERTAINMENT OPTIONS

From blackjack and craps to roulette, poker, and other specialty games, Bally's Casino has 36 gaming tables and more than 1,200 slot machines. The casino offers patrons a complimentary Commodore Club Card that allows guests to receive rewards while playing the slot machines. The casino also holds slot tournaments, birthday extravaganzas, craps and blackjack tournaments, and other prize giveaway events.

In addition to gaming, Bally's Casino entertains guests biweekly with nationally known musicians and comedians. The Wildcard Sports Bar, located in the main lobby, seats 100 guests, features 16 television screens showing sporting events, and has a 100-square-foot megavision screen. *Belle of Orleans* has two additional sports bars. And the Washington deck, located on the first level of the riverboat, can accommodate up to 625 guests for private parties and receptions.

When dining, guests can choose from more than 60 entrées at the Great American Buffet. The all-you-can-eat restaurant offers a variety of cuisines that include Cajun, Creole, and old-fashioned American cooking. There is also the Liberty Bell Deli, with operations both landside and aboard the boat.

GIVING BACK TO THE COMMUNITY

Bally's Casino credits the community and loyal employees for making the casino a success. After hiring more than 700 local employees, the organization takes pride in a very low turnover rate. "We focused on hiring local people," says Roscoe N. Greene, senior vice president of operations. "We are definitely the largest employer in New Orleans east."

The casino has helped strengthen the local economy as well. Bally's Casino pays more than $25 million in state and local taxes. The casino also annually purchases $23 million worth of various goods and services from the local community. "We're a significant part of the city's budget because of our contributions," Greene adds. To further its impact on the community, the casino contributes to numerous organizations and local universities, such as United Way, United Negro College Fund, United Cerebral Palsy, University of New Orleans, Southern University at New Orleans, Xavier University, and Dillard University.

In the future, Bally's Casino hopes to develop the property at South Shore Harbor by adding additional amenities to its operation. "We just look forward to being part of the New Orleans community in the coming years," Greene says. "We're the only riverboat in New Orleans, and we appreciate the loyalty of both our customers and our staff." ●

INCE 1995, TENET HOSPITALS OF NEW ORLEANS HAVE met the needs of hundreds of thousands of patients through innovative and creative programs. The seven local Tenet Hospital campuses—located in Jefferson, Orleans, and St. Tammany parishes—employ more than 5,000 people, and provide health services to citizens of 13 parishes and three Mississippi counties.

TENET'S SEVEN LOCAL CAMPUSES

Memorial Medical Center, the largest private health care provider and teaching hospital in the Greater New Orleans area, is a full-service hospital with two separate campuses. Following the 1994 merger of Southern Baptist Hospital in Uptown and Mercy Hospital in MidCity, the two historical hospitals were renamed Memorial Medical Center when they became part of Tenet HealthSystem in 1996.

Memorial Medical Center offers a broad range of services from obstetrics to solid organ transplantation. Memorial's specialized programs and services include an American Diabetes Association (ADA)-accredited Diabetes Management Center, Bloodless Medicine and Surgery Program, Breast Center, Epilepsy Institute, Kidney Dialysis Program, Leukemia Program, Blood and Bone Marrow Transplantation Program, Rehabilitation Institute of New Orleans, StrokeCare Early Intervention and Treatment Program, and the Transplant Institute of New Orleans. The hospital also provides a Women's Center; Perinatal Diagnostic Center and Unit for high-risk pregnancies; and a Level III Neonatal Intensive Care Unit.

In the fall of 2001, Memorial opened the area's newest facility, the New Orleans Surgery and Heart Institute, on the Baptist campus. This institute combines technologically advanced surgical and cardiac facilities and a skilled staff under one roof.

St. Charles General Hospital, located in the heart of the Garden District, was founded in 1971 to meet the needs of a small, sophisticated Uptown community. Today, the hospital offers high-level care that stresses personal attention. The hospital's specialty programs include a weight management center and a hyperbaric chamber for the treatment of wounds. St. Charles General Hospital also offers a nursing home liaison program, a skilled nursing unit, and a sleep lab.

Doctors Hospital of Jefferson, built in 1984 in Metairie, specializes in cardiovascular, orthopedic, general medical, and surgical services. The hospital also provides 24-hour emergency services, a full-service operating room, an open-heart surgery program, rehabilitation services, and a skilled nursing facility.

Kenner Regional Medical Center became a Tenet hospital in 1995. The full-service hospital is affiliated with Louisiana State University's Orthopedics and Family Practice programs. In the fall of 2001, Kenner Regional opened TenetCare, a new facility that provides outpatient and same-day services in an environment completely focused on customer service.

Tenet also provides health care to patients across the Mississippi River and Lake Pontchartrain.

Meadowcrest Hospital was built in 1984 to meet the needs of a growing west bank population. The general medical and surgical acute care facility offers comprehensive medical services.

NorthShore Regional Medical Center, a full-service acute care facility located on a 100-acre campus in Slidell, was built to meet the needs of residents on the north shore of Lake Pontchartrain.

As the Greater New Orleans area continues to grow, Tenet Hospitals of New Orleans are one step ahead. Tenet's local hospitals continue to distinguish themselves as leaders in redefining health care delivery and being recognized for providing quality, innovative care to patients in the Greater New Orleans area. ●

SINCE 1995, TENET HOSPITALS OF NEW ORLEANS HAVE MET THE NEEDS OF HUNDREDS OF THOUSANDS OF PATIENTS THROUGH INNOVATIVE AND CREATIVE PROGRAMS.

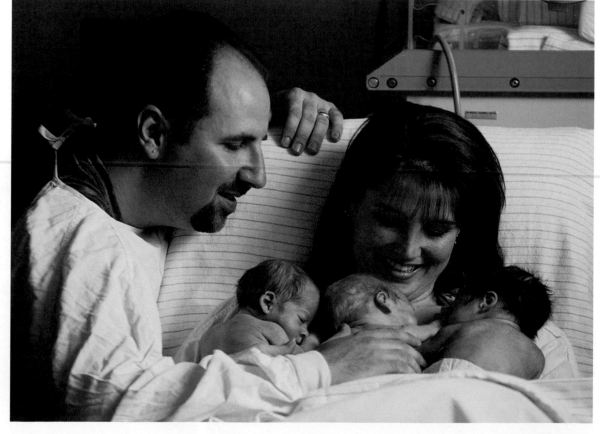

NEW ORLEANS IS ONE OF AMERICA'S OLDEST SOUTHERN CITIES—RICH in history, culture, and ambience. With a strong sense of community, improving crime statistics, and a growing economy spurred by tourism, the city of New Orleans is drawing back former residents along with an influx of new ones. These are positive signs in a city that has faced many public health challenges during the last century.

However, unlike most parishes in Louisiana, New Orleans has a local public health department— the Healthy New Orleans Partnership is supported by the city's health department. With a goal to improve the health of residents, the partnership brings these groups together with a collaborative Community Health Improvement Plan, which focuses on individuals, families, and the community, while placing children as a priority.

A HISTORY OF CHANGE

Founded in 1997, the Healthy New Orleans Partnership was formed to become "the change agent of the public health system." The partnership, which was created with a vision and desire for a healthier New Orleans and an improved public health system, is composed of more than 75 groups and organizations representing local and state government, universities, health care and school systems, neighborhood groups, community agencies, churches, and individual citizens.

The Healthy New Orleans Partnership spent much of its first 18 months strengthening the organization's capacity and focusing on the planning process. Monthly meetings, a citywide health summit, and a daylong action planning retreat prepared partners for a series of more intensive, consensus-based workshops that took place from May through December 1999. During these workshops, which involved more than 220 stakeholders, the partnership developed a comprehensive visioning process, a conceptual framework for the public health system, and a consensus on 17 recommendations for community public health system improvements. The partnership is currently focusing on these community improvements.

WORKING FOR ADVANCEMENT

A centerpiece of Healthy New Orleans Partnership's plan is the development of the Center for Empowered Decision Making. As the partnership's working arm, the center will host collaborative planning, anthropological research, neighborhood-level data collection on health issues, and community participation in decisions.

Other primary work areas include institutionalizing an expanded definition of public health to include quality-of-life issues; developing community health networks through which community leaders and neighborhood residents train and work with health professionals on health issues; developing community capacity to participate in public health policy development; and monitoring and evaluating best practices in service delivery.

Founded out of need, the Healthy New Orleans Partnership is becoming a integral part of the health care of New Orleans' residents. Constantly striving to fulfill its mission, the partnership will continue to define its role in the city for decades to come. ●

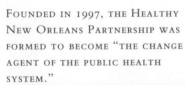

FOUNDED IN 1997, THE HEALTHY NEW ORLEANS PARTNERSHIP WAS FORMED TO BECOME "THE CHANGE AGENT OF THE PUBLIC HEALTH SYSTEM."

ESTLED ADJACENT TO BAYOU SEGNETTE STATE PARK ON Segnette Boulevard, and located only minutes from New Orleans' central business district and the historic French Quarter via the Crescent City Connection Bridge, the John A. Alario Sr. Event Center is the premier sports and event facility in Westwego. Opening its doors in 1999, the Alario

Center—designed to be a multipurpose facility and amateur sports complex—is rapidly becoming the hub of social and cultural activity on the west bank of the mighty Mississippi River. The center is a joint venture between the State of Louisiana, Jefferson Parish, and Louisiana Superdome.

HOSTING LOCAL, NATIONAL, AND INTERNATIONAL EVENTS

From high school graduations and basketball and volleyball games to weddings and baby showers, the Alario Center provides a facility for locals to showcase their most important events. The center also hosts trade shows, church events, arts/crafts shows, theatrical performances, concerts, carnival balls, and fund-raisers. "The Alario Center serves as a community center," says Blake J. Dardar, general manager. "It is the only facility like this on the west bank."

In addition to hosting local community events, the Alario Center

sets the stage for numerous regional, national, and international sporting events. The men's and women's U.S. Olympic Weightlifting Trials, a nationally televised event, was held at the center on July 22, 2000. The winners of the event competed in the 2000 Olympics in Sydney.

The center has also hosted girls' basketball tournaments, with teams competing from countries ranging from Puerto Rico to Finland. And paint ball competitions have brought teams together from as far away as France and England. "We have the ability to bring an international audience to the community," Dardar says.

The Alario Center held roughly 300 events in 2000, compared to 160 events in 1999. The increase in the number of events has meant an increase on the center's economic impact on the community. "From an economic standpoint, we're able to bring people to the west bank, put them in our hotels, get them in our restaurants, have them shop at our malls, and have

them visit our tourist attractions," Dardar says.

MAKING JEFFERSON PARISH A BETTER PLACE

One of the unique features of the Alario Center is its 30,240 square feet of column-free, maple-hardwood floor space, as well as its 2,400 theater-type seats. "I don't think you'll find anything of that type in the state," Dardar adds.

The facility has 12 full-time employees, an on-site caterer, a full-service kitchen, and three concession stands, as well as three meeting rooms totaling 4,657 square feet. The center recently constructed a state-of-the-art baseball stadium. Future projects on the drawing board are a softball quad and soccer fields.

"The opening of the Alario Center in 1999 was in line with Jefferson Parish President Tim Couloun's message, 'Jefferson, a better place,'" Dardar says. "We definitely think this center has helped make Jefferson Parish a better place." ●

NESTLED ADJACENT TO BAYOU SEGNETTE STATE PARK ON SEGNETTE BOULEVARD, AND LOCATED ONLY MINUTES FROM NEW ORLEANS' CENTRAL BUSINESS DISTRICT AND THE HISTORIC FRENCH QUARTER VIA THE CRESCENT CITY CONNECTION BRIDGE, THE JOHN A. ALARIO SR. EVENT CENTER IS THE PREMIER SPORTS AND EVENT FACILITY IN WESTWEGO.

BEGINNING AS A SMALL PUBLISHER OF LOCAL NEWSPAPERS IN 1935, Towery Publishing, a division of Baretz Publishing, LLC, today has become a global publisher of a diverse range of community-based materials from San Diego to Sydney. Its products—such as the company's award-winning Urban Tapestry Series, business directories, magazines, and Internet sites—continue to build on Towery's distinguished heritage of excellence, making its name synonymous with service, utility, and quality.

COMMUNITY PUBLISHING AT ITS BEST

Towery Publishing has long been the industry leader in community-based publications. In 1972, current President J. Robert Towery succeeded his parents in managing the printing and publishing business they had founded four decades earlier. "One of the more impressive traits of my family's publishing business was its dedication to presenting only the highest quality products available—whatever our market might be," says Towery. "Since taking over the company, I've continued our fight for the high ground in maintaining this tradition."

During the 1970s and 1980s, Towery expanded the scope of the company's published materials to include *Memphis* magazine and other successful regional and national publications, such as *Memphis Shopper's Guide*, *Racquetball* magazine, *Huddle/FastBreak*, *Real Estate News*, and *Satellite Dish* magazine. In 1985, after selling its locally focused assets, the company began the trajectory on which it continues today, creating community-oriented materials that are often produced in conjunction with chambers of commerce and other business organizations.

All of Towery Publishing's efforts, represented on the Internet at www.towery.com, are marked by a careful, innovative design philosophy that has become a hallmark of the company's reputation for quality and service. Boasting a nationwide sales force, proven editorial depth, cutting-edge graphic capabilities, ample sales and marketing resources, and extensive data management expertise, the company has assembled the intellectual and capital resources necessary to produce quality products and services.

In 2001, Towery became a wholly owned subsidiary of The Oxford Companies of Chicago. Oxford, which employs some 7,000 people, makes equity investments for itself and its investors, and owns companies in health care, commercial finance, telephone, and publishing industries.

URBAN TAPESTRY SERIES

Towery Publishing launched its popular Urban Tapestry Series in 1990. Each of the nearly 100 oversized, hardbound photojournals details the people, history, culture, environment, and commerce of a featured metropolitan area. These colorful coffee-table books spotlight communities through an introductory essay authored by a noted local individual, an exquisite collection of photographs, and in-depth profiles of select companies and organizations that form the area's business core.

From New York to Vancouver to Los Angeles, national and international authors have graced the pages of the books' introductory essays. The celebrated list of contributors includes two former U.S. presidents—Gerald Ford (Grand Rapids) and Jimmy Carter (Atlanta); boxing great Muhammad Ali (Louisville); two network newscasters—CBS anchor Dan Rather (Austin) and ABC anchor Hugh Downs (Phoenix); NBC sportscaster Bob Costas (St. Louis); record-breaking quarterback Steve Young (San Francisco); best-selling mystery author Robert B. Parker (Boston); American Movie Classics host Nick Clooney (Cincinnati); former Texas first lady Nellie Connally (Houston);

TOWERY PUBLISHING PRESIDENT J. ROBERT TOWERY (LEFT) TOOK THE REINS OF HIS FAMILY'S BUSINESS IN 1972, MAINTAINING THE COMPANY'S LONG-STANDING CORE COMMITMENT TO QUALITY.

STEVE DAVIS

JONATHAN POSTAL/TOWERY PUBLISHING, INC.

JONATHAN POSTAL/TOWERY PUBLISHING, INC.

SORTING THROUGH HUNDREDS OF BEAUTIFUL PHOTOGRAPHS IS JUST ONE OF THE ENVIABLE TASKS ASSIGNED TO TOWERY'S TOP-NOTCH TEAM OF DESIGNERS AND ART DIRECTORS, LED BY AWARD-WINNING CREATIVE DIRECTOR BRIAN GROPPE (LEFT). MEMBERS OF TOWERY'S EDITORIAL STAFF CULL THE BEST FROM MATERIALS SUBMITTED BY FEATURE WRITERS AND PROFILE CLIENTS TO PRODUCE THE URBAN TAPESTRY SERIES.

and former New York City Mayor Ed Koch (New York).

While the books have been enormously successful, the company continues to improve and redefine the role the series plays in the marketplace. "Currently, the Urban Tapestry Series works beautifully as a tool for enhancing the image of the communities it portrays," says Towery. "As the series continues to mature, we want it to become a reference source that businesses and executives turn to when evaluating the quality of life in cities where they may be considering moving or expanding."

CHAMBERS OF COMMERCE TURN TO TOWERY

In addition to its Urban Tapestry Series, Towery Publishing has become the largest producer of published and Internet materials for North American chambers of commerce. From published membership directories and Internet listings that enhance business-to-business communication, to visitor and relocation guides tailored to reflect the unique qualities of the communities they cover, the company's chamber-oriented materials offer comprehensive information on dozens of topics, including housing, education, leisure activities, health care, and local government.

The company's primary Internet product consists of its introCity™ sites. Much like its published materials, Towery's introCity sites introduce newcomers, visitors, and longtime residents to every facet of a particular community, while simultaneously placing the local chamber of commerce at the forefront of the city's Internet activity. The sites provide newcomer infor-

mation including calendars, photos, citywide business listings with everything from nightlife to shopping to family fun, and on-line maps pinpointing the exact location of businesses, schools, attractions, and much more.

SUSTAINED CREATIVITY

The driving forces behind Towery Publishing have always been the company's employees and its state-of-the-art industry technology. Many of its employees have worked with the Towery family of companies for more than 20 years. Today's staff of seasoned innovators totals around 120 at the Memphis headquarters, and more than 40 sales, marketing, and editorial staff traveling to and working in an ever growing list of cities.

Supporting the staff's endeavors is state-of-the-art prepress publish-

ing software and equipment. Towery Publishing was the first production environment in the United States to combine desktop publishing with color separations and image scanning to produce finished film suitable for burning plates for four-color printing. Today, the company relies on its digital prepress services to produce more than 8,000 pages each year, containing more than 30,000 high-quality color images.

Through decades of business and technological change, one aspect of Towery Publishing has remained constant. "The creative energies of our staff drive us toward innovation and invention," Towery says. "Our people make the highest possible demands on themselves, so I know that our future is secure if the ingredients for success remain a focus on service and quality."

JONATHAN POSTAL/TOWERY PUBLISHING, INC.

WITH *The Open Container*—AN OUTDOOR SCULPTURE BY MEMPHIAN MARK NOWELL—MARKING THE SPOT, TOWERY'S MEMPHIS HOME OFFICE SERVES AS THE HEADQUARTERS FOR THE COMPANY'S INNOVATIVE, COMMUNITY-BASED PUBLICATIONS.

Library of Congress Cataloging-in-Publication Data

New Orleans : proud to call it home / introduction by Pete Fountain ; art direction by Bob Kimball ; sponsored by the Young Leadership Council.
    p. cm.
  ISBN 1-881096-89-0 (alk. paper)
  1. New Orleans (La.)—Pictorial works. 2. New Orleans (La.)—Civilization. 3. New Orleans (La.)—Economic conditions. 4. Business enterprises—Louisiana—New Orleans.   I. Fountain, Pete. II. Kimball, Bob. III. Young Leadership Council.
  F379.N543 N49 2002
  976.3'35—dc21

2001005333

Printed in China

Towery Publishing, a division of Baretz Publishing, LLC,
The Towery Building, 1835 Union Avenue, Memphis, TN 38104

www.towery.com

Publisher: J. Robert Towery **Executive Publisher**: Jenny McDowell **Sales and Marketing**: Carol Culpepper, Gingo Spencer, Kim Wade **Sales Manager**: Bill Koons **Project Directors**: Linda Berman, Connie Boudreaux, John Carver, Susan Diehl, Lynette Molin, Kristi Palermo **Executive Editor**: David B. Dawson **Managing Editor**: Lynn Conlee **Senior Editors**: Carlisle Hacker, Brian L. Johnston **Project Editor/ Caption Writer**: Danna M. Greenfield **Editors**: Rebecca E. Farabough, Sabrina Richert, Ginny Yeager **Profile Writer**: Tara Smith **Creative Director**: Brian Groppe **Photography Editor**: Jonathan Postal **Production Manager**: Laurie Beck **Profile Designers**: Rebekah Barnhardt, Glen Marshall **Photography Coordinator**: Robin Lankford **Production Assistant**: Robert Parrish **Scanning and Color Correction**: Eric Friedl, Darin Ipema, Mark Svetz, Rusty Timmons, Bill Towery **Film Production:** Jeff Burns, Michael Burns, Jamey Johnsen **Print Coordinator**: Beverly Timmons

FOTO

PHOTOGRAPHERS

Steve Baker is an international photographer who has contributed to more than 100 publications. As the proprietor of Highlight Photography, he specializes in assignments for clients such as Eastman Kodak, Nike, Budweiser, the U.S. Olympic Committee, and Mobil Oil, which has commissioned seven exhibitions of his work since 1994. Baker is author and photographer of *Racing Is Everything*, and he has contributed to numerous other Towery publications.

The preeminent chronicler of Louisiana's Carnival cultures, **Syndey Byrd** was one of eight photographers featured in the PBS special *Ten Thousand Eyes*. Her cultural vision has been honored with numerous gallery exhibitions and a one-woman show at the New Orleans Museum of Art, and her images have appeared in magazines and books.

After 10 years as a lighthouse keeper in the Irish Lighthouse Service, **Richard Cummins** relocated to Southern California and taught himself photography. He has exhibited at galleries in Ireland, San Francisco, and Palm Springs, as well as in Rockefeller Center and the United Nations headquarters in New York. His images have been published by *National Geographic*, *Sierra*, and *Practical Photography*, and have appeared in several Towery publications.

Owner of Fineart Photography, **Alex Demyan** places a strong emphasis on travel photography, particularly subjects related to Louisiana and Mississippi. His clients include the Louisiana Office of State Parks, Jefferson Parish Public Schools, and the New Orleans Publishing Group, and his images have won awards from *American Photo Magazine* and *Popular Photography*.

Rosemarie A. Doumitt, who has worked as a freelance photographer and a teacher of fine art black-and-white photography, specializes in dance, travel, and prenatal subjects. Her images have appeared in the *Times-Picayune* and in work commissioned by the New Orleans Ballet Association and other organizations and individuals.

An art director at Towery Publishing, **Enrique Espinosa** earned a bachelor's degree in art history from Rhodes College. He has done freelance photography for various Memphis-based and regional firms, and his images have appeared in numerous other Towery publications.

Lee Foster, a veteran travel writer and photographer, has had his work published in major travel magazines and newspapers. He maintains a stock library that features images of more than 250 destinations around the world.

Founded in 1991, **GeoIMAGERY** is a membership association of photographers, writers, travelers, and natural history enthusiasts. Composed of a group of photographers with a common interest in exploring the world photographically and developing publishing outlets for these images, GeoIMAGERY has grown to more than 200 members, with diverse styles producing broad coverage.

A freelance photographer, **Marlene Goldman** concentrates on adventure and cultural travel photography. Winner of the 1999 Book Passage Travel Writing Award, she also won the Best in Show, Best Animal Photo, and Best People Photo at the 2001 Western Chapter meeting of the Society of American Travel Writers.

Owner of Stephen Graham Photography, **Stephen Graham** specializes in architecture, interior design, people, lifestyle, and landscape photography, as well as aerial, stock, corporate portraiture, and rural and city images. His work has appeared in publications by A.M.D.G. Architects, Campbell/Manix, Commonwealth Cultural Resource Group, Lerner Publications, Owl Creek Productions, Voyageur Press, and University Business Interiors.

Founded by Jim Baron in 1986, **Image Finders** is a stock photography company located in Cleveland, Ohio. Its files cover a broad range of subjects, including agriculture, animals, butterflies, families, food, sports, transportation, travel, trees, and the western United States.

After studying art in his native Ireland, **James Lemass** moved to Cambridge, Massachusetts, in 1987. His specialties include people and travel photography, and his images have appeared in numerous other Towery publications.

Originally from Bay St. Louis, Mississippi, **Ken Murphy** owns Studio South II and South Coast Publishing. Specializing in advertising and landscape photography, he enjoys photographing scenes for calendars and books, and has published images featuring coastal Mississippi.

Originally from Gulfport, Mississippi, **George Payne** has lived in the New Orleans area for nearly 10 years and has a strong interest in natural world photography. His images have appeared in *Shutterbug*, *Louisiana Life Magazine*, and *Soundings*.

A graduate of Tulane University, **Earl Perry** owns FotoPerry and specializes in music performance, authors, motor racing, and New Orleans area photography. His clients include the House of Blues, New Orleans Superdome, Indianapolis Motor Speedway, and Peter Max, and his images have been published in *Elle*, *AutoWeek*, *Gambit*, and *OffBeat*. He has covered the Indianapolis 500 for more than 20 years, as well as any and all book-signing events for novelist Anne Rice.

Photophile, established in San Diego in 1967, has more than 1 million color images on file, culled from more than 85 contributing local and international photographers. Subjects range from images of Southern California to adventure, sports, wildlife, underwater scenes, business, industry, people, science and research, health and medicine, and travel photography. Included on Photophile's client list are American Express, *Guest Informant*, and Franklin Stoorza.

Anthony Pidgeon is a house photographer for San Francisco's Fillmore Auditorium and freelances for several local and national publications. He has had images featured in numerous books, calendars, travel guides, and CD and promotional packages.

Franco Rossi is a freelance photojournalist whose specialties include travel, fashion, interior, and editorial photography. He has contributed images to such publications as *Capital*, *Elle*, and *Cosmopolitan*.

A curator for several local art exhibitions, **Katherine Scherer** works for the Arts Council of Greater Baton Rouge and focuses on arts administration and photography instruction. She was the principal photographer for the CD insert of WWOZ-FM's *Sounds of New Orleans—Volume 8*, and she has served as a panelist for the Louisiana Endowment for the Humanities' publications and photo documentary grants.

Specializing in travel and nature photography, **Kay Shaw** is the owner of Kay Shaw Photography and is widely published in books, magazines, newspapers, and calendars. Originally from Minneapolis, she has traveled most of the United States and to 29 countries.

Originally from Baton Rouge, **Warren Smith** specializes in night photography and imaginative window displays. His client list includes such shops as Fleur de Lis, Limbo, Fifi Mahony's, and Importico.

Owner of Strout Photography, **Jeff Strout** specializes in fashion, commercial, celebrity, and special events photography. His clients include the TCI Companies, Verizon Wireless Corporation, the Audubon Institute, New Orleans Ballet Association, the Arizona Diamondbacks, Saks Fifth Avenue, and Tommy Boy Music.

Originally from the New Orleans area, **Joni S. Whittington** is a freelance photographer who is currently indulging her lifelong passion for photography at the New Orleans Academy of Fine Arts.

Other contributing photographers include Carol D. Hunt. For further information about the photographers appearing in *New Orleans: Proud to Call It Home*, please contact Towery Publishing.

INDEX OF PROFILES

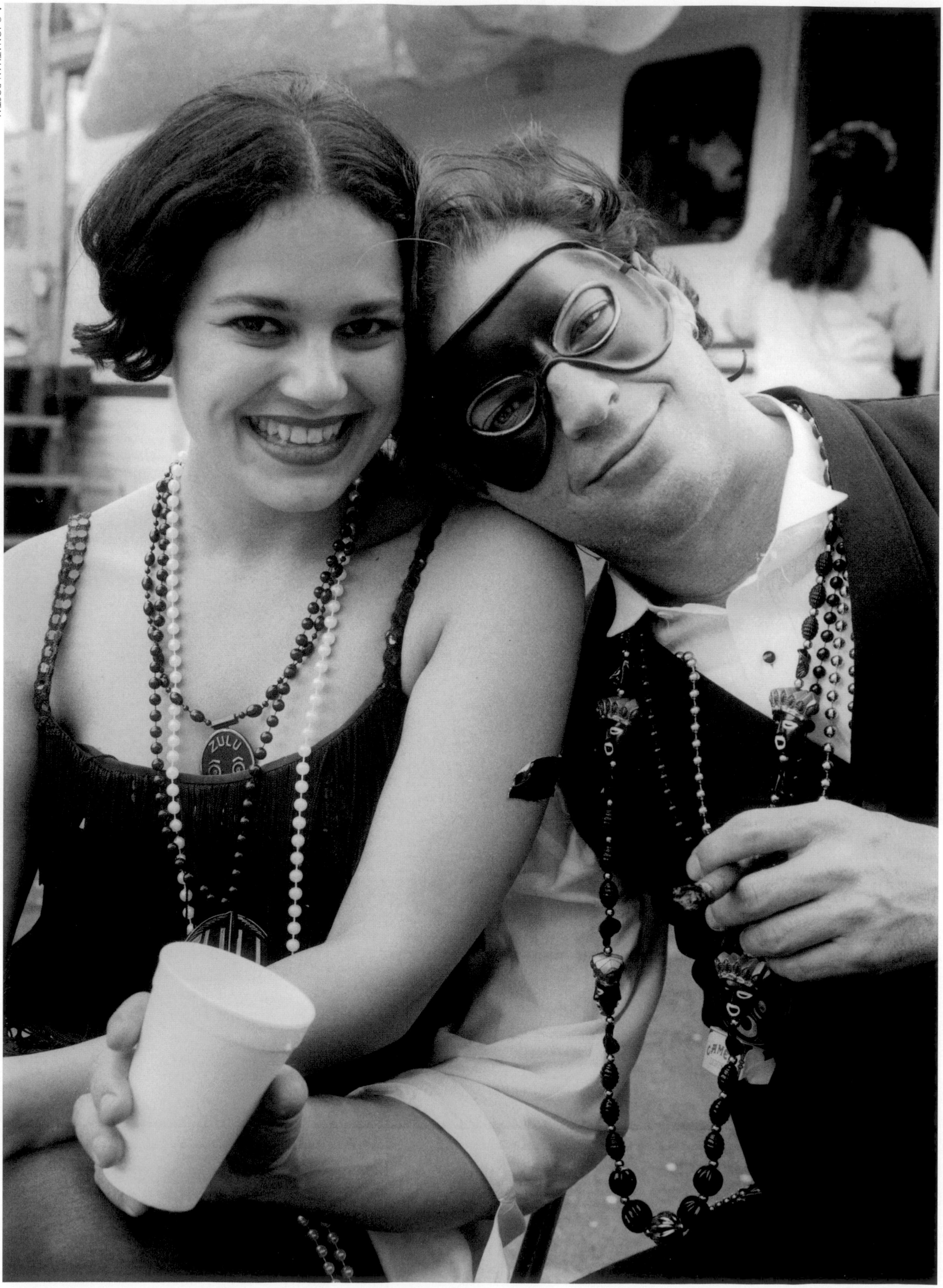

▲ © JONATHAN POSTAL